Companionship

A Private or Group Book, About Dating, Courtship, Engagement and Marriage

Bill E. Carter

This book is a work of non-fiction. Unless otherwise noted, the author and the publisher
make no explicit guarantees as to the accuracy of the information contained in this book
and in some cases, names of people and places have been altered to protect their privacy.

LifeRich Publishing is a registered trademark of The Reader's Digest Association, Inc.

LifeRich Publishing books may be ordered through booksellers or by contacting:

LifeRich Publishing
1663 Liberty Drive
Bloomington, IN 47403
www.liferichpublishing.com
1 (888) 238-8637

Because of the dynamic nature of the Internet, any web addresses or links contained in
this book may have changed since publication and may no longer be valid. The views
expressed in this work are solely those of the author and do not necessarily reflect the
views of the publisher, and the publisher hereby disclaims any responsibility for them.

Any people depicted in stock imagery provided by Getty Images are
models, and such images are being used for illustrative purposes only.
Certain stock imagery © Getty Images.

ISBN: 978-1-4897-2886-9 (sc)
ISBN: 978-1-4897-2885-2 (hc)
ISBN: 978-1-4897-2887-6 (e)

Library of Congress Control Number: 2020907036

Print information available on the last page.

LifeRich Publishing rev. date: 04/30/2020

Companionship

A <u>PRIVATE</u> OR <u>GROUP BOOK</u>, ABOUT DATING,
COURTSHIP, ENGAGEMENT AND MARRIAGE

A PERSON CAN READ THIS BOOK WITH PRIVACY!
FOR ADULTS AND TEENS.

Self-Published by: Bill E. Carter
Editors and Proofreaders:
Mary Salmon, Bill Carter, (and a new friend)

<u>CONTACT INFORMATION: BILL E. CARTER:</u>
billcarter2005@yahoo.com
Bill E. Carter, PO BOX 1602, Owensboro KY 42302 USA

Bill has worked in IRAQ as an ARMY CONTRACTOR

Have some fun with this group book.
Share with your friends and talk about the subjects within
this book. I assure you; it will cause some laughter.

Contents

A note from the writer: there are a few phrases that are redundant so you can retain the information. Please use this as a **GROUP BOOK**. This is one of the greatest books ever written to interact and have fun within a group of people.

Introduction

Bill, had a column called, **"TODAYS CHRISTIAN SINGLES"**. He has studied and written many topics on single adult's issues. **A BOOK FOR YOUTHS, PARENTS, SINGLE ADULTS, *STUDENTS* AND *MILITARY PERSONNEL*. (Chaplin's Office)**

This book, *"Companionship"*, is detailed so that an adult can sit down and read it in privacy, to allow a person to think about relationship issues. Parents can sit down with their teenagers and go over the detailed issues of dating. The teens can read this book on their own.

This book can bring a person into a new level of maturity and understanding of relationship skills. This book on dating topics gives a person an understanding of why a relationship can or cannot work. It includes a path for a great marriage and how to avoid a divorce. It also teaches people how to leave a relationship, that will not work out, as friends, instead of a broken relationship or a broken heart!

The five-basic principles of building a relationship, (time, trust, truth, faith, and friendship), is explained in this book. There is information on the four temperaments to help a person understand character and personality issues while dating. People will learn the difference between dating and courtship. The last part of this book covers basic sex education to help protect people from unwanted pregnancy and STDs.

This book can be used as a group book for discussions, advice from parents, a guide book for adolescents, single meetings, church programs, and military relationship education classes. This book offers reality with maturity to all who read this book! The contents of this book are rated: <u>**RM, for (Reality with Maturity)**</u>.

Bill was in Iraq as an Army Contractor for 37 months. He has seen and observed our soldiers talking about issues they were having within their relationships. Most young and older adults could increase their understanding of relationship skills by reading this book.

If you can afford to buy this book, *"Companionship"*, or even a few cases, please send one or a few books to our soldiers, addressed to a **Military Chaplain's Office of any base.** Please do not forget we have bases both nationally and internationally. This book will easily fit into a soldier's backpack. As a soldier reads this book, it may very well bless and give them the hope and desire to become a better person and the confidence of having a real relationship.

This book has facts and opinions that I hope make people **RETHINK** their **THOUGHTS** on **DATING!** *When I use the word (I) in this book, it only represents what I have seen, took notes, asked questions within a large age group, heard from people in the single's ministry programs, my studies and courses, over a ten-year time period.*

PART 1

Know What You Want

SINGLE ADULTS & TEENS, ARE IN A SPIRITUAL BATTLE

Dating should be filled with good intention, yet I often wonder why dating was like entering into a conflict. Most adults will learn that dating is much like a spiritual battle. Dating is only one step away from walking into a battle zone which can lead a person into an emotional battle. Dating is hard for single people. Single adults (*young and old*), tend to make so many mistakes while learning to date in order to find that someone special. I've learned that dating does not have to be a conflict. I've also learned that dating mistakes exist from the following areas: **Being immature, not having people skills, life management skills, and last but not least, relationship skills.**

Single people do not need to be judged by other people. Adults know when they have made a mistake. What single adults need to do is to recognize their faults and learn from them. This would give single adults some understanding and knowledge and to allow a person to grow and mature. Did you know most people will not mature until late in their life?

Being mature is not by age! *It's about the skills of life you learned to use and come to appreciate. I will introduce the four temperaments, later in this book, so a person can understand themselves and others a lot better.*

If you are seeking a long-term relationship, a person must know what they want out of a relationship! Yes, I'm asking that you take the time to write down what you want out of a person, in order to have a long-term relationship.

People do not think about what they want out of a relationship, why? Most people while dating take a path of destruction and never learn to take a journey. **Walking on a path is like taking the same old trail. Taking a journey is like making plans to go somewhere.** So, let's start the **JOURNEY**!

The following is what I would want out of a relationship with a person that could lead to a long-term relationship and maybe marriage. Here are a few things I came up with to make you think! I also wrote my thoughts into this to make you think sincerely! When people do not think, they will do anything, even if it's wrong. You got to know what you want in order to have it, right? **Look at these 12 issues, and be open-minded.** The straightforwardness of this writing is to make you **RETHINK** issues within **RELATIONSHIPS** and **PEOPLE SKILLS**.

<u>1: SOMEONE THAT UNDERSTANDS COMMUNICATION SKILLS:</u> Here is one of **Mark Twain's quotes:** *"I never seen so many men with tongues so handy and information so uncertain"*! I would not date a person that just verbalize anything to make themselves look good or think they know something when they do not, that's not being mature. People need to learn that communication skills are about 75 % listening and 25% speaking. If a person cannot be a listener, then, that person is nothing more than a broken recording of nothings. Why, because they cannot hear enough to learn life skills!

When couples cannot learn to talk or have speaking skills, that same pair is going to have a relationship of verbal **expression of nonsense**; count on that! **Most arguments extend from COMMUNICATION SKILLS;** either by not learning to speak properly or not learning to listen and retain information. Never tell a person, always share information with them. Remember, no one wants to be told what to do. Never forget to ask a question if you didn't understand what was said. If a person is speaking vainly, question that person. (Who, What, When and Where, should be involved in are speaking skills.)

Never, take anything for granted. There is nothing in communication skills that is written in stone! *If one person in the relationship has communication skills and the other doesn't, then there has to be a learning time for the one that doesn't or the two will have an unpleasant relationship.* Here is something I said and believe. "If a person cannot control their thoughts and the way they speak, more than likely they will not control their mind either!" All single adults need to think about this last statement. Within speaking skills never call a person a name or play the blame game. This will in time kill a relationship or keep it from healing.

2: I WANT A PERSON TO BE MY FRIEND, THAT LEADS TO BEING A BEST FRIEND. Here is one of my previous writings with new changes that I think would be best to incorporate into this book.

LOVE, NEVER COMES BEFORE FRIENDSHIP! What does it take to become friends? People need to spend a lot of time getting to know one another. This is the beginning of building a friendship, and then comes trust. How long should it take a person to trust someone? My answer is: from a few months to a lifetime! Trust brings us to truth, which brings us to faith, which builds a foundation for friendship to be built on.

Allow me to introduce the five principles of relationship development that I had to learn. **TIME, TRUST, TRUTH, AND FAITH THAT BRINGS FORTH FRIENDSHIP.** Then, there are levels of friendship. Let's start at the beginning to see how two people can become friends and keep away from just being strangers!

TIME: Using your time wisely brings forth wisdom in relationship development. People may think they must see each other every day, but that is not the case. The relationships that stand the test of time, are the ones in which each person gives the other space.

You do not need to smother each other. When you smother something, it dies! It's the same in relationship building. How much time do you need before you feel you can trust someone? Remember you have all the time in the world (actually the rest of your life).

TRUST: What does trust mean to a person in a real relationship? This is what I found when I looked at the definition of trust in my dictionary: to depend on, to put one's confidence in another person.

How many times have you put your confidence in another person and been let down? What do you think was the cause? **Maybe you did not give yourself enough time to trust or they weren't trustworthy.** Nevertheless, time helps us to understand trust!

Assured reliance on the character of a person must be built from a time frame that allows two people to really get to know each other's character. Friends must trust with the assurance that they can depend on each other. How long does it take you to trust someone? How long does it take for someone to trust you?

How often have you heard people say, *"TRUST ME"*? **You will have great tribulations if you take that statement for granted!** I never make that kind of statement. Why, because I can't control all the things that might go wrong to keep me from fulfilling what I said. I do not say, **"Trust me,"** because I have chosen to walk in truth and I want you to walk in truth as well. **A man and woman should walk together with truth that is centered on trust!**

TRUTH: Genuine, honest, sincere, actual, reliable, able to be trusted, *rather than having false pretense.* **Concerning relationship development, before truth can set you free, truth must inform you and change you.** To have truth takes time and trust.

Truth should lead a person to information on why they should change. It took me a long time to learn to walk in truth. Here is a great question for today's single adults; do you think people should walk in truth? My question is, why don't they?

FAITH: Belief, trust. Faith is always active: It is a commitment of both the mind and heart! My view of faith in relationships; is a product of trust that can only develop with time and knowledge. People are not taught to have faith in a relationship. With faith, a person learns to care for themselves and the other person. Most people never understand the value of having faith in a relationship. Without faith, it's impossible to have a great loving relationship. Any relationship without faith is doomed. Faith is more than life skills and it should be.

FRIENDSHIP: People must first become friends to have a real friendship. What is a friend? I will share my definition. A friend is not just an acquaintance. Acquaintances are people you come in contact with. A person may know someone by name; however, they don't really know that person. They may be coworkers, neighbors, social contacts, church members, even family members. They may be "friendly," but that is not the same as being a friend.

If a person says they are my friend and is only an acquaintance, I am the first to recognize this because I safeguard my association, with my real friends. I do this to protect myself! You will never have to boast about a real friendship. The signs of caring will be obvious!

FRIEND: What is a friend like? A real friend is affectionate, caring and loving. They will respect, admire, value, and appreciate you for who you are, not what they want you to be. They will have regards for you and respect you positively. They are also willing to be accountable to you. A friend does not pull you into mistakes: lie, steal from you, use you, call you names, try to control you, disrespect you, take advantage of you, smother you, place a title on you, own you, say one thing and do another, or refuse to be accountable for their behavior! A friend does not depend on you to meet all their needs. False friends are not givers and seldom help you even when they could.

3: <u>**LEARN TO BECOME A BETTER PERSON**</u>: This took me a long time to understand in order to change and develop a quality relationship, instead of being a stranger or a person that would not change to become a better person.

<u>Truth</u>: Truth keeps us from getting into trouble, making mistakes, having unrealistic expectations, and indulging in vain imaginations. I revealed something to myself a long time ago that changed the course of my life. I think it will change the course of people reading this subject as well. (**Before truth can set you free, truth must inform you and change you!**) We must know what truth is, to keep us from a dreadful relationship or marriage. If we seek truth first, we will avoid the pain that comes when a relationship does not work.

NINETY-NINE PERCENT OF ALL RELATIONSHIPS WILL NOT WORK! But the good news is that it only takes one person to have a lifetime of courtship, love, commitment, companionship, and marriage. We must learn to understand when a relationship will not work. Keep your journey alive in order to fine that right person. People must learn to count it as a blessing when they have a break up in a relationship. A person can allow this life lesson to teach them the truth within relationship skills. This should motivate a person to keep searching. When we find that one person, we will have the truth, knowledge, and wisdom we need in order to have a loving relationship.

KNOWLEDGE: This is a lifetime pursuit. Very few seek knowledge and the consequences are severe for those who don't. Here is a quote from the book of Hosea 4:6 "My people are destroyed for lack of knowledge; because thou hast rejected knowledge..." **Most of our problems stem from a lack of knowledge!** There's plenty of information out there, but too many people reject it. If a person wants a lasting relationship, they must seek knowledge about the skills of life, life management skills, family skills, people skills, team skills, and of course relationship skills.

Mankind should not be dumb, stupid or ignorant! Whether a relationship works out or not, knowledge of relationship development will be a blessing to you. Lack of knowledge destroys a relationship and leaves a person hurt, brokenhearted, and often in denial. Knowledge will show people the truth and restore their confidence, but a lack of knowledge will produce jealousy, conflict, a desire to control and then we make more mistakes not knowing we are making them.

4: <u>TO BE A COMPASSIONATE PERSON:</u> I want this to be known about compassion. Trust and truth and faith, will always support compassion. What is compassion? Most people do not understand compassion. My view of compassion: It's a person that has a beloved feeling for people or a person, they have mercy, kindness, humility, meekness, and they understand long suffering. A person with compassion will bear someone's burden, they forgive one another and they certainly do not judge people or a person. But above all these things they have and will show signs of love, which is the bond of perfection. **A person with peace allows compassion to rule their hearts.**

People will never have true love or companionship, without compassion! If a person takes compassion out of a relationship what will reinforce love? To be a companion a person must have compassion! *What does compassion mean to you?* Compassion is many things. It is not only sympathy. It is being concerned about the one you love, doing what is needed without being asked, and understanding when someone is having a bad day or a hard time. It is giving and understanding with love during these times and really being there for someone in both the good and bad times. Compassion builds up people and relationships. It encourages morality in a relationship and it inspires motivation.

I am speaking now as a man and from a man's point of view. As men, we need to show more compassion in our relationship with a woman! Women must learn to understand that it is not always easy for a man to be compassionate or even to know when to show compassion. There are some women and even more young adults, today, who don't have compassion.

Compassion is learned and people must learn to use compassion with their loved one if they want a fulfilling and deeply caring relationship! **Just like love, compassion can and will teach us to become a better person!** Too often, we do not understand this because we have not been taught to have compassion!

5: <u>CHANGES WITHIN A RELATIONSHIP:</u> Men and women, it's up to you to grow and learn to become mature! **You do not need someone to ask or share with you to become more mature!** You may think that's a little annoying. I've seen too many people in the workforce, who have the evidence of being immature and irresponsible! I know this to be true! I had to man up and I suggest that you as a person do the same! This would make life easier for everyone, within all your relationships and marriage! **People do not want a person who will not change or who is immature!**

We all know that life is filled with changes, and so are relationships and marriages. If you want a lasting relationship that is full of love you will have to face many changes as the relationship develops. **ADULTS NEED TO TAKE THIS SERIOUSLY:** If a person cannot accept changes or someone is not willing to change, the relationship will stop growing. It will not reach the stage of companionship either. **There is no point in having a relationship if a person is not willing to face and take on the needed changes for it to survive and thrive! How many relationships have gone down the road of no change, just to face another dead-end?**

Over the years, I have seen too many marriages die because the husband and wife were not willing to change! Most dead marriages end up in divorce and if the couple stays together, they may live in a state of being miserable. **Changes are needed before you get married, and with a great relationship and marriage, there will be a lot of changes!**

No one needs to tell an adult the changes they need to make in their bad habits or behavior and character. **So, don't be offended if the person who loves you, and is in a relationship with you, points out a needed change! They are only trying to have more quality within the relationship!** We don't have the right to control anyone. Changes must come from within a person. We can only change ourselves, not anyone else! *When and if, you become offended, what did you learn?*

Habits, behaviors, and character traits, will no doubt take time to change. Nothing happens overnight and it can take a few weeks to see changes. I know I have areas in my life that need changing. We all do. One of the most important steps in my life was to understand myself and search for the adjustments I needed in order to make my life greater! You may need to take this into consideration as well! When you are willing to change, you are on the road to improving yourself and your relationship development. **WE STOP MATURING WHEN WE STOP SEEKING KNOWLEDGE ABOUT LIFE!** Maturity takes some human intervention (sometimes a trusted counselor) and some human effort (you!). Of course, people must first realize that they need to make changes.

6: <u>**EVERYONE NEEDS TO HAVE AN UNDERSTANDING OF THEIR OWN PERSONAL HYGIENE.**</u> Without quality in your personal hygiene, how would a person expect someone to be near them? Take a bath once a day or two if you need it! Brush your teeth, and look clean. Your attire brings forth an attitude so dress as good as you can, by all means!

Men, do not run around in your work clothes. One of my female friends stated this, "Men do not know when they look bad or dirty". That is a good point to bring up! **Women, people should not forget to keep up their appearance**. Do what you can to stay as attractive as you were when the relationship began. I know we all change as we grow older but it's up to couples to stay in shape!

MAKE A NOTE OF THIS: Then there are housekeeping issues. Keep your house and home clean! When you are a single person the other person looks at how well you have kept the bathroom and kitchen areas clean. This is a sign of who a person is!

7: <u>**NOT BEING EQUALLY COMPATIBLE**</u>: This subject of not being equally **COMPATIBLE** has brought forth more issues in trying to have a relationship than anything else. **PEOPLE MUST BE COMPATIBLE.** Sometimes I've tried to force a relationship to work. Like the song goes, "**WRONG**", that was a mistake, within my relationship building and this was a life lesson well learned!

Eventually, a person feels they have been deceived when they find that a relationship or dating does not work. But the truth is, people create their mistakes by not using knowledge and wisdom! **Being unequally compatible, keeps two people in a false relationship that has been built with expectations and hopeless imagination.** People get hurt the most when they want a relationship that is not based on **compatibility!** Think about some of your past relationships that were not **compatible**?

What does unequally **compatible** mean to you? Most single adults never think about this when they're considering having a relationship. This one area of being *__unequally compatible__* is the cause of most bad break ups and failed relationships! You know by now the five qualities that go into relationship building. **Even with the best intentions, you cannot have a relationship with just anyone!**

In all relationships we need to understand that it takes a labor of love to keep that relationship alive and healthy. We, as adults, should put quality time into a relationship because it takes that to bring out the truth. Time will show the men and women, if they are *unequally compatible* with one another. To be unequally matched means you have no real connection with the other person. In light there is no darkness and in darkness there is no light. **If you know at the start you are unequally matched, then by no means should a person go out with this other person! That's like taking on a torment, and that in itself is the wrong thing to do!**

We know, of course, that the most important thing to have in a relationship is faith. After that there are areas of compatibility that makes building a relationship easier. Are you and the other person close in age, appearance, and education? Do you have similar people skills? Are you shy or outgoing? Do you agree on financial issues, goal-setting, and time management? Can the man and woman walk in commitment? Do you share the same desires, and needs? Are you both willing to be accountable for your actions and to each other?

Is gaining knowledge, understanding, wisdom and maturity of equal importance to each of you? What do you think about falling in love or growing in love? What about the subjects of sex, drugs, alcohol, and STDs? Do both the man and woman have a greater understanding about these very important issues? Do you and the person you want to build a relationship with, have the understanding that change is necessary to achieve harmony? Where do you stand and can you stand together? **I think you get the illustration, if not, "all hell will break lose in a relationship".**

8: <u>**UNDERSTANDING THE FOUR TEMPERAMENTS:**</u> I am going to list for you the four types of temperaments. These categories have come from one of my pastor's teachings and my own Internet research. There are tests on the Internet that a person can take to find out what their temperament is. **I really suggest having a certified counselor or pastor do this test with you.**

<u>**I AM NOT A COUNSELOR**</u>, but I think you will benefit from the insight I have included here. People don't often understand themselves, much less others. This, of course, leads to the misunderstandings that can or will break up relationships and marriages. It's the man's and woman's responsibility to find that area of agreement within their temperaments.

Temperament tests are used in marriage counseling and I would take one before I got married! Everyone is different and knowing these four temperaments could save a person from having bad break ups and heartbreaks / depression. In every relationship, there are unique differences. Have you faced some? Do you have unique differences?

Temperaments: A prevailing or dominant quality of mind that characterizes someone's excessive moodiness, irritability, or sensitivity, and the quality of the mind resulting from various proportions of the four cardinal humors in somebody. Sanguine, choleric, melancholic, and phlegmatic.

Sanguine: *The sanguine temperament is fundamentally impulsive and pleasure-seeking; sanguine people are sociable and charismatic.* They tend to enjoy social gatherings, making new friends and tend to be boisterous. They are usually quite creative and often daydream.

Some alone time is crucial for those of this temperament. Sanguine can also mean sensitive, compassionate and romantic. Sanguine personalities generally struggle with following tasks all the way through, are chronically late, and tend to be forgetful and sometimes a little sarcastic. Often, when they pursue a new hobby, they lose interest as soon as it ceases to be engaging or fun. They are very much people persons. They are talkative and not shy. The sanguine generally have an almost shameless nature, certain they believe what they are doing is right. They have no lack of confidence.

Sanguine: *The not so great Characteristics.* Vanity and self-complacency, loving the appearance of his/herself and the praise of others. The sanguine is very inclined to flirt, and has a great degree of jealous tendencies. The sanguine cannot be left alone (*they get lonely*). There is cheerfulness and a love of pleasure that accompanies the desire to always have someone around to enjoy life with. Sanguine decisions are likely to be the wrong decisions. Their undertaking fails easily because the sanguine believe success is inevitable and will therefore take it for granted. They are unstable, and they have little understanding of themselves since they rarely internalize conflict.

Choleric: *The choleric temperament is fundamentally ambitious and leader-like.* They have a lot of aggression, energy, and or passion, and try to instill it in others. They can dominate people of other temperaments, especially phlegmatic types. Many great charismatic military and political figures were choleric. They like to be in charge of everything. However, the choleric also tend to be either highly disorganized or highly organized. They do not have in-between setups, only one extreme to another. As well as being leader-like and assertive, the choleric also fall into deep and sudden depression. Essentially, they are very much prone to mood swings.

Choleric: *The not so great Characteristics.* The choleric is commonly prideful, full of themselves, thinking highly of their great qualities and even considers their faults worthy of praise. Also, is stubborn and has an opinion on everything. The choleric believes they are always right. The choleric is confident, believes others are weak, ignorant, incompetent and slow. Upon humiliation the choleric feels hurt resulting in anger, deceit, and judgments towards others.

Melancholic: *The melancholic temperament is fundamentally introverted and thoughtful.* Melancholic people often were perceived as very (or overly) pondering and considerate, getting rather worried when they could not be on time for events. The melancholic can be highly creative in activities such as poetry and art and can become preoccupied with the tragedy and cruelty in the world. Often, they are perfectionists. They are self-reliant and independent; one negative part of being a melancholic is that they can get so involved in what they are doing they forget to think of others.

Melancholic: *The not so great Characteristics.* Easily falls into mental distress and this can be extremely intense. The melancholic, more than any other temperament, has keen awareness of moral right and wrong, and has a deep longing for morality. They are inclined to despair, intense expressions of grief, and occurrences of depression. This can result in self-pity, and they may become a burden to friends and family. They can also lose confidence in others, specifically superiors. There is a loss of trust and respect when the melancholic becomes aware of a fellow man's weaknesses and faults. The melancholic vehemently desires justice, and forgiveness of offences is hardly an option. They are suspicious, lacks trust in people and fear that everyone is out to get them. They are pessimistic about everything.

Phlegmatic: *The phlegmatic temperament is fundamentally relaxed and quiet, ranging from warmly attentive to lazily sluggish.* The Phlegmatic tend to be content with themselves and their kind. They are accepting and affectionate. They may be receptive and shy and often prefer stability to uncertainty and change. They are consistent, relaxed, calm, rational, curious, and observant, qualities that make them good administrators. They can also be passive-aggressive.

Phlegmatic: *The not so great Characteristics:* Inclined to things that require little to no effort, eating, drinking, is lazy, and neglects duties. Often misses opportunities, has no ambition and no aspirations in life.

Now that you have read the four temperaments, you will probably **have an idea of which is your most dominant temperament.** It's possible you may also have characteristics of other temperaments. These give us insight into the personality differences in both men and women. It takes about 60 to 120 days to recognize a certain temperament, and it is often at this point that some couples crash. One of two things typically happen. The couple tries to work through the differences, or they call it quits. Friends will go through this period with understanding and respect for each other. This is why building friendship should be important! *Do you think that real friends work through their temperaments? They should and will have to!*

If you cannot work through the temperament part of a relationship, it's best to stop the relationship at that point. **<u>NEVER DISRESPECT ANYONE, JUST MOVE ON!</u>** This is where we find people who are quick to say, "I love you," but in a few weeks or more, will be saying, "I hate you." This comes from a lack of knowledge! The people who use the statement, "I hate you", concerning a relationship break up, may never understand or attempt to learn temperaments or relationship development. People have the right to be who they are and if you do not like their temperament move on and remain friendly. Should we hate people, are we taught to hate, and can a person teach them self to hate? (*A reality question; does hate keep a person and their mindset from reality?*) (*What has hate done for you?*)

There are a lot of adults who will never have an understanding of their own temperament, much less someone else's. They want to rush into a make-believe relationship so they can fall in love without the foundation of relationship development, which **includes TIME, TRUST, TRUTH, FAITH, AND FRIENDSHIP.**

I want to caution you here. Be cautious with people who fall in love quickly. On the other hand, there are men and women who seem to go further in relationship building when they take in the understanding of their own temperament. Some even have a great long-term relationship due to this understanding of temperaments. They are able to work through these temperaments with patience.

9: **<u>THE COST OF A RELATIONSHIP</u>**: Relationship within a budget has helped me to have more activities and learn to work within a budget. **The man and woman, in any relationship will have to address the issues of cost in having a relationship.** I have learned that every relationship has a cost. As you read this subject you will find what I have learned and want to share with you as a single person. It's about the expenses in a relationship. Some people are fortunate to have extra money for activities. Others may have created a solitary lifestyle because they think it takes a lot of money to be in a relationship, and they are right!

As you get to know one another in a relationship, you should share expenses! If a person pays all the expenses, they may come to think something is due to them. There are people who think they can buy love. On the other hand, the person who always receives may feel as if they *do* owe the other person something. **An unbalanced financial situation, can set people up for failure in building a relationship.** Sharing expenses will help both the man and woman, to learn how to budget. Forming and working within a budget will help couples to bond. This is an important part of relationship development for both the man and the woman; adolescents need to learn this important life lesson as well!

I know what it is to have financial problems after a divorce. Men and women can both have money problems after a marital break-up or a cohabitation break-up, but they can still have fun in a relationship if they learn to share the expenses of a relationship.

We all know, it costs to go out. Maybe someone doesn't have that much to spend, so consider the different things you can do and still stay within your budget. Your first financial priority is your own money management. You already know that if you don't work, you don't eat. If you don't manage or budget what you do earn, you may not be eating either. If there is to be any extra money for activities in a relationship, a budget is a necessity.

It may sound old-fashioned, but walking in the park has a lot going for it. It is time well spent, talking and getting to know one another, laughing, seeing nature and exercise and it's all free. Money was just as tight in the *"old days"*. A lot of loving relationships have developed by walking in the parks. Take a cooler and sit at a park table. (***Here's a hint:*** Men, Women think having a picnic is exciting and so should men!) It's also a low-cost way for the two of you to have some quality time together and really get to know each other while having a meal in the park and taking in a conversation. Women like for men to talk and share in a long conversation. This may sound funny and, in my opinion, talking is part of the glue that holds a relationship together!

Sometimes, I have driven out to the country to find a spot by a lake, creek or river. It's a great place to sit on the tailgate of your truck and have a picnic. **Men, most women like walking in nature and just talking to a** man. It's peaceful and that's *precious!* Some great moments have come from sitting on a hillside, looking at a lake, river, or valley. Men, pick some wild flowers for your lady friend. Once away from the noise of the city and its crowds, you'll find the calmness and peace that's much healthier for both of you and the relationship.

10: **WE NEED HOBBIES:** Every couple needs a hobby or a few hobbies and couples can have hobbies together. This is one area in a relationship that can help save a working relationship. *We must learn that it takes a lot of work to keep a relationship alive as we walk through the labor of love.*

Learn to take a break from one another or giving each other space, this is a good way to allow the relationship to *reset* **and** *rest.* Each couple should have their own hobbies, and I also would encourage couples to find a hobby that both, can take interest in. I want to include a previous column I wrote a few years ago, called, *"THE MAN CAVE"*, to give some insight to how hobbies can help.

THE MAN CAVE

Being a single man, it seems like my home, shop and camper at my river lot, is a man cave. However, I really enjoy spending time with my lady friend in these so-called man caves. I just bought my first sign that states "Man Cave", but what does it really mean? As a writer, I search for facts about statements and sayings. Its 5:30 in the morning and I am writing this column from my river lot (camper), the Man Cave so to speak. I realize that there are times that a man and woman need to be alone or spend time apart from each other, and this is a good thing!

I also know that I do not want to make my Man Cave a place where a woman cannot come into the arena, that would be sad in itself! A man is not meant to be alone, that is why God created a woman for the man.

So, what is a Man Cave? Is it just for the man, I hope not, for I enjoy the presence, of a woman! Perhaps it's a place where a man can work on his stuff. I noticed that my lady friend enjoys working in my shop with her stuff she sells at one of the local flea markets. My shop is full of tools and supplies I use in my small business. She gets a kick out of using the Man Cave. So, I noticed that the man cave is a welcome area for a woman as well! I like to watch her work or just hang around.

Then there's my camper with a sign in the window that states Man Cave. But I noticed I have more fun when she visits. We cook, go hiking, boating, fishing, kayaking, go for long drives, sit on the patio overlooking the Ohio River and talk away the day.

I am glad that God made a woman for a man to keep and have great company with! My man caves are open to my lady friend and it should be even if you're married! I hope that men will learn something from this column.

A woman seeks a man as much as a man seeks a woman. The fact is that man does not know how to let a woman into their Man Cave (life) and enjoy the presence of a woman.

So, is the Man Cave an expression of men saying they do not know how to have a relationship? I really think so! The more the man learns to involve the woman, the greater the friendship grows in that relationship. Is that true? Sure, it is! Then a real love develops and is kept alive when the man and woman involve one another in their lifestyle and hobbies.

What happens when men and women become involved in one another's hobbies or activities? They become more in tune to building a greater relationship. I was at the point where I didn't use my shop other than, for my small business. But my lady friend likes art. I knew nothing about art. But this past year I started to do some art, I call it folk art.

I painted my interior shop door with an eagle, bigfoot and the end of the trail painting of an Indian praying on his horse. I started to sale my paintings at Rough River State Park in Kentucky, did my first art show, and I really enjoyed that. I took the money I made from the art show and donated it to one of the homeless shelters here in Owensboro.

All of this happened, because I allowed my lady friend into my Man Cave. Men, women are a blessing, if you have a so-called man cave invite your lady friend or wife into the cave and allow her to be a part of your life! Who knows what can happen if a man would allow a woman to be a friend and to become their best friend! Men we need to learn this life skill from a statement that God himself stated, *"It is not good that the man should be alone; I will make him a help mate (woman) for him"*!

11: <u>**DATING TO COURTSHIP:**</u> At the start when people meet, they should just go out, without calling it a date. This will take the pressure off of meeting someone new! ***Allow a few weeks (12 weeks), to pass before you say you are dating.*** Take the time to see if you want to hang around with this new person. Hold back and be restrained from being physical. Ask and talk about STDs. This may demonstrate the level of a person's immaturity or how mature a person is. Seek to see if the person you're going out with, talks like an adult, if not, leave that person. Let's all be adults that have actions of an adult.

Courtship is something I should have known; this is something that I learned later in my life. Courtship is understanding a relationship with a commitment. I know that the word courtship has been lost in our vocabulary within this modern time. Within this word "**COURTSHIP**", it has taught me to understand relationship development and taught me to understand what a working relationship was about. There are a lot of differences between dating and courtship. It is best to go out with one another for a while before dating or courtship, perhaps a few weeks. This allows both of you a chance to see if you have a real interest in one another and can build friendship. Getting to know each other is what going out or a date should be about! **If it does not work out, count it a blessing; learn this teaching as part of your life management skills!**

It is sad, but most people that end a relationship of dating leave the relationship without being friends. That is not the purpose of dating is it? Today's relationships can be compared to jumping into deep water without knowing how to swim. When the current gets too strong, they give up and drown; or when their temperaments clash, they crash. Courtship is like wearing a life jacket. It keeps you afloat while you work through the temperament of one another. You can survive courtship and still come out being friends. *Even if the relationship doesn't work out, you should remain friends!* *Why can't people remain friends when the relationship doesn't work out? Most of the time, it's because couples never develop a friendship-based relation and they lack the understanding of life skills!* **Note this: people have the right to break up at any time.**

What is the difference between dating and courtship? I am glad you asked. **Courtship offers commitment!** Courtship searches for truth in relationship development. If the courtship ends, two people can still be friends. Courtship gives the couple the opportunity for a man and woman to build a relationship, based on **relationship skills**. Courtship may and can develop a loving relationship that works toward engagement and marriage. Today's society accepts dating as a way of life with all its heartbreaks. **Dating offers no commitment!** It is simply an appointment to go out or to get to know someone for the most part. **The problem with dating is people do not engage in relationship development, while courtship takes on the** effects of relationship development! Which would you want to endure, Dating or Courtship?

I want to encourage this. People that are trying to find a partner to become a couple, they need to go out on a few dates before jumping into the courtship box? This will give you a chance to see the social skills, you two display. This also checks a person's, people and relationship skills. Look and listen when they speak or ask a question this will give you an understanding of their mindset.

12: <u>SOMEONE THAT CAN NOT CONTROL THEIR EXPECTATIONS AND IMAGINATIONS:</u> I am going to add here part of a previous column I wrote to point out why it's important to live within reality.

EXPECTATION: This area of our behavior, can cause people a lot of problems. Within our expectation, there is an anticipation of something happening; a confident belief or strong hope that an event will happen. When we have a notion, a mental image of something expected, we should frequently compare this to reality. With the right expectation comes the truth. We must learn to control this behavior. Our anticipation of our expectation can and will cause us to be misdirected. This can cause a great deal of disappointment. I have seen people whose minds were disordered by this issue of expectation.

This is when expectations will cause you to have a problem with your mental state, mindset, and relationship building. Confusion starts here as people step outside of the box of reality. When you allow a desire to become a false hope, you are not in control of your mindset. If we do not learn to control our expectations early in life, a person will have a hard time with this as an adult. This is often done without understanding all of the information of truth. Relationships can be and have been destroyed over one's expectation.

IMAGINATION: This is where we have the ability to visualize and to form images and ideas in the mind, especially things we have never seen or experienced. One's imagination can be both good and bad, for it is the creative part of one's mind. This is one area of the mind where we can have created resources, like the ways to deal with difficult problems. In this area, we can resolve problems and repair things, but this area of imagination must be developed. One's imagination must be used in a controlled way and within reality! When we allow our imagination to take over, we can have thoughts and fears that take over. Sin can be found in imagination. One's imagination can lead to depression. If you don't control your imagination who will?

Children have their parents to help instruct their use of imagination. This is a part of childhood. As adults, we are influenced by outside sources that are not real role model images, of having a good life from the entertainment world, media and other sources. These areas of life and behaviors will cause you to make mistakes. This can and may take a person down a dead-end road that has no reality. It has been said so many times that sin, mistakes, and problems, start with our imagination. When we get committed to a thought of imagination, is it for good or bad? We are not born to be a bad person; we are taught to be bad people. Yes, you can teach yourself to become a bad person. We are born in hope of having good values that give us the gifts that come with understanding. We must watch over and safeguard our association with people and influences.

Expectation and imagination, will affect your relationship. It can build or destroy peoples, love, companionship, and even marriage. I have seen this happen too many times. Here is a good illustration; a man gives a woman a rose, does he love her or was he just being kind?

PART 2

Managing the Relationship

<u>WE ALL HAVE A FREE WILL</u>

We as Americans, born in the land of the free, have a right to free will and no man or woman can change that! What does that mean in a relationship and in dating or courtship? A person has no right to control or own a person! Many people have tried to control people while in a relationship. This is nonsense and if a legal line is crossed, a person may face legal action. **NO ONE HAS A RIGHT TO TELL OR MAKE A PERSON DO ANYTHING! SO, LEARN TO ASK AND LISTEN TO THE ANSWER!**

I have seen relationships where a person controlled the other person, even when you're married you still do not have a right to enslave a person! Before you go out with someone, talk to that person about this control and free will issue. Then learn and understand from the other person for all the right reasons.

We do not need to have anyone else hurt while trying to find the right person to fulfill one's life; do we? If a person, for whatever reason, chooses to stop seeing someone, they have that right! If you disagree with this, step out of the dating game! Do not become a foolish person! Learn who the other person is first, before dating!

When you meet someone new, use this time to come to know that person. I give a strong warning here; do not get physical at this point. Take the next 30 days to talk and see if there might be an opportunity of having a relationship. Allow me to make this clear, you have the rest of your life to have sex and if that is what they want move on. Sex doesn't build a relationship does it?

This leads to another subject within this topic; the two of you should talk about Sexually Transmitted Diseases (STDs). I would bring this up as an adult at the start of going out. Why, one may ask? 30% or more of adolescence and adults, have or had a STD's. With that said, find out and seek the truth! There are some STD that cannot be healed. This type of STD will always remain a part of the person who has that STD that they can't get rid of, sad but so true! (You can look up STI, sexual transmitted infection.) I just want you to have an understanding.

Check their personal issues like how many times they been married, how many children they have, divorces, jail time, crimes, and finances. Do they have behavior issues like being bi-polar, PTSD, and any other mental condition? *We all could learn something about these issues, so, why not talk about it?*

This may take a few weeks for a person to open up to share this type of information, but ask the needed questions. Women you may have to lead on this issue. Men do not talk openly and they think it's a weakness. Men, push your pride aside and tell the truth, this goes for the women as well.

If you do not ask questions, then you will more than likely say, **"WHY DIDN'T YOU TELL ME"**! Men and women, you are adults, ask all the questions you can think of. **Get the facts before you give them your heart!** You may laugh at this but if you do not get the facts, you're going to cry sooner or later! **So, start talking, if they do not want to talk, this is a sign to move on, isn't it?**

ONE'S BODY LANGUAGE

I'm including information from a column I wrote. To help you understand that there are signs people give in their body language that would save a person a lot of time, effort and possibly the hurt of a broken relationship.

I have an understanding of body language, perhaps from my walk in this life. Not only can this save you from trouble, it should be notice in the first stages of a relationship. This may keep a person from a bad relationship. **We all have body language, let's not overlook this anymore! Body language:** The gestures and mannerisms by which a person communicates with his or her body. Body language can show signs of behavioral problems. Body language can also show signs of quality behaviors.

I want to make everyone aware that body language is part of the structure of a person. Body language allows you to see a person for who he or she really is. When body language goes along with one's communication skills at the beginning, you are looking at a person who is being his or her true self. If one's body language is different from one's communication, there is a reason for that and this should give you a warning sign!

At times people will use their body language before they use their communication skills. When a quality person has good body gestures, it shows. When a person has aggression in his or her body language, this will show also and give you the first sign of trouble. Body language will happen before poor communication skills (for the most part). Everyone can speak nicely, but most people don't control their body language due to a habit-forming reaction. Most people do not teach themselves how to control their body language!

Signs that someone is aggressive: Hitting things, pointing fingers, holding up their hands a lot, faking hitting things (including people), kicking things, fake kicking, grabbing, biting their lip/tongue, fingers, and so on. These are just a few signs. Most people who have aggression in their body language have real habits of using gestures. **THESE HABITS CAN BE A WARNING AND SHOULD BE**! People that are (Drama Queens), have a lot of body language and this should be noted as well!

Signs that someone has quality behaviors: Hugs, handshakes, looking at you when he or she talks with happiness or understanding, waves, smiles, makes signs of peace, looks like he or she is listening. Do they have eye contact and show signs of peace? Look at how peaceful people act and respond within their body language. These are just a few signs we as single adults should recognize and so should teenagers!

You have to spend time with someone to understand their body language. That's another reason to take your time in a relationship. It may take 30 to 90 days for a person to notice someone's body language. How many mistakes in relationship building could be avoided by observing someone's body language? I have found that if I take the time to look at someone's body language, this could and will, save me a lot of time and trouble. I also took notice of my own body language. This has helped me to improve my people skills. Learning body language is just as important as communication skills. Controlling my body language has helped me change my character. That was also a lot of labor.

I have watched people over the years and I have concluded that one's body language should be observed before getting involved in a friendship, relationship, and marriage.

Think back about your body language in past relationships. **If you take the time to learn your body language, it will help you to control your emotions and behaviors. This is true for everyone!** Without judging, think also about the other person's body language in your past relationships. What does it tell you about that person? Can you recall from their body language what was going on before some issues became verbal or apparent?

If a person is not in control of their body language, they will or may have emotional reactions that may become verbal or physical. *Never make fun of someone's body language. It's a part of their emotional make up and character! You can ask them about their body language, but only if you are ready to take on a person's emotion, behind the gestures. A friendly person does not use bad body language, do they?*

JEALOUSY

Mindset: A set of beliefs or a way of thinking that determines behavior and outlook. **Imagination:** The ability to form images and ideas in the mind, especially of things never seen or experienced directly.

People that come from a strong family structure are taught by their parents not to be jealous or envious. These parents spend a great deal of time teaching their children this important lesson. There are other parents who did not come from a strong family structure who did not put much time into teaching these same life skills to their children. **There are people who never took the opportunity to understand why they are jealous.**

Jealousy is a part of our personal and emotional make up. It can grow quickly in a destructive imagination mindset. Jealousy stems from feelings or emotions, fear, and lack of confidence, knowledge, trust or faith.

Some people have a very difficult time controlling their emotions. Jealousy does not come from a sound mind, but from fear or control. Single adults should not live within the spirit of fear or control, but a spirit of peace, love and a sound mind. Controlling our emotions takes self-discipline. **Either you are in control of your mind or your mind is in** control of You. Jealousy can destroy a relationship if a person allows their mindset or emotions to be ruled by their thinking and emotional behavior.

You cannot have a great relationship if you have jealousy issues! It will affect the person you are dating, courting or married to. **Jealousy is no more than an out-of-control behavior that extends from one's imagination!**

If a person is dating someone and the other person finds someone else that they are attracted to and they want to go out with another person, give them your blessings. That last statement may be hard to understand. **Nevertheless, people have a right to freedom!** Like all of us, we are searching for someone to have a relationship with. Here is what a person should do when a relationship comes to the end of the road. Remain friends with that other person. There is no reason to be upset with them and their new acquaintance or yourself.

When relationships do not work out for whatever reason, single adults should understand that a break up is usually in their best interest. I hope everyone who reads this book learns that it only takes one right person to have a relationship with. **Single adults should focus on searching for that right special person with all their heart, shouldn't they?** This is why single adults and teens need to learn this life lesson and learn also to control their emotions.

Living with jealousy will waste a person's time and give them a dreadful and frightful personality. Jealousy will create mental issues if not contained! Single adults and teenagers do not need the bad personality traits of jealousy. People will recognize the character within a jealous person sooner or later, and for that reason they may not have anything to do with this type of person! Single adults and teenagers should look for a mature person with a sound mind! We as single adults need to understand what this paragraph is teaching! This should be understood as a word of warning! Do not go out with a person who has a mindset of being a jealous person!

We all should recognize that 99 percent of dating and relationships will not work out. This should build your confidence in who you are and why you should save yourself for the right special person!

There is no jealousy in knowledge, wisdom, or joy. Jealousy is a tormenting spirit or mindset that can and will bring forth legal issues, mistakes, mental behaviors and sin. Jealousy will most likely end a relationship and destroy any trust or love that has been established. *Friends should never be jealous of one another.* If you don't trust someone, do not go out with them. It's as simple as that.

* NOTE THIS: Everyone needs to know that a person is looking for a mate that they want to be with! We all have that understood, right? If people would take on the mindset, of thinking that they need to be the <u>right person</u> for the <u>other person</u>, could this bring understanding into the rim of dating and help <u>prevent jealousy</u>? **How could we learn to stop jealousy?** *<u>Perhaps if we would talk about jealousy at the start of seeing someone, this might help.</u>*

Are you the right person for the right relationship?
A question you should answer, before getting involved.

REVENGE

Perhaps this is another reason I wrote this book, people may or can become revengeful, within one form or another. This is a life lesson that should be taken to heart and seriously. **WHICH IS WORSE, JEALOUSY OR REVENGE?** A lot of men and women have experienced both. **REVENGE IS A DARK SIDE OF JEALOUSY!** Sometimes even a good person can snap and take revenge from a broken relationship. We, as single adults and teenagers, should learn not to think about or plan revenge after a break-up. NOTE: A break up is no more then, *it didn't work out!* We must learn to just walk away. *It didn't work out, should not take away from your courage of trying to fine the right relationship.*

<u>Adults and teenagers are not capable of handling revenge!</u> As a person trying to find the right special person, we must learn to displace vengeance. The Bible states that vengeance belongs to God alone. Revenge puts a person in a mental state that may keep them from controlling their physical and mental behavior. A person who dwells on revenge can lose self-control. Revenge produces foolish and reckless behavior – stalking, threatening, and injury to others. Certainly, a sound-minded person does not want to do those things!

People get into the mentality of revenge because their emotions are out of control and they may think it's the only way to keep or repair a relationship. Maybe they decide it's the only satisfaction they can get because the relationship is ending. **REVENGE HAS NO PLACE IN RELATIONSHIP DEVELOPMENT!**

A person who is caught in acts of revenge face public exposure and embarrassment when their actions are brought out in the newspapers and media. That person may also face criminal charges and the consequences that go with them.

Who and how many others will get hurt if you are determined to take revenge? Stop and think, a person could lose their job and could face imprisonment. This type of person *will* lose their self-respect and any respect that others may have had for them. If a person ever feels strongly about taking revenge, seek counseling. **The attitude of revenge is a spiritual battle that will hurt others after it first hurts the person in such a *mindset*!**

We all have issues after a broken relationship. Sometimes they are for the wrong reasons. I recognize it's hard to understand the end of a relationship if you have had your own expectations or imaginations! How should single adults and teens, handle a relationship break-up? **As hard as it might be, face the truth, the truth will inform you! This may sound unrealistic in today's world, but this is an important principle to apply and to learn not to seek revenge!**

Isn't it better to end a relationship with a blessing than revenge? Bless without the expectation of someone coming back into the relationship. Here is where single adults make mistakes that lead to revenge. Someone has skipped the five basic steps of relationship development; I know this is a repeat, but one that is worth understanding and applying in today's single lifestyle!

Expectations can be good or bad. I like to address the bad type of expectation. **Bad expectations come from thoughts that do not see the other person or the relationship realistically!** These expectations are, more or less, a form of make-believe and similar to **"DAY DREAMING"**. They set up the **"dreamer"** and maybe the other person to be embarrassed and hurt when they believe what they are hoping for can and will happen. Nothing good will come from this type of expectation! **Good expectations should be a joint reality; one that is agreed on by both the man and the woman!**

When people are controlled by their imagination, they have entered into a spiritual battle! This is where we see real harm being done to other people – date drugs, date rape, jealousy, revenge of all types, including the possibility of murder. A person may try to do something he or she has imagined because he or she is not controlling their mind. We live within a time of anger in America, with revenge racing through countless minds.

We are living in a generation that supports violence on TV, in movies, and in games. We have become selfish, prideful, addicted to alcohol, drugs and involved in gang membership. The faith of our Christian values is disappearing. **In my opinion, more than 60 percent of teenagers and adults in America support violence.** Because of that, they are filled with a self-made anger that can lead to madness, and a temporary form of insanity. By allowing their imagination to be filled with these ungodly thoughts, they have stopped loving, caring about, and forgiving others.

Listen to and observe carefully the person you are seeing. **When people speak aggressively, or talk about hurting others this should be a red flag to you; take this as a warning sign!** Leave these types of people alone, by all means, do not get involved with their actions! **People who try to control other people have no respect for others or a loving relationship!** Stay away from that type of person. They do not accept counseling very well because they are not willing to change the thoughts that would change their behavior. They act foolishly and for the most part they are immature in relationship development. Usually, they also lack self-confidence.

My thoughts, to stop revenge, a person may have to train themselves to handle the pain or hurt, which may come from wanting something that they cannot have.

PART 3

Having Fun

HOLDING HANDS, it sounds so simple and is in many ways. Please do not hold hands until you feel something for that other person. The following is one of my past columns I wrote. Holding hands should not happen until trust has been established. Holding hands is full of body language. I have watched older couples at the parks or events as they held hands; I am talking about married people that have stood the test of time! They embrace their hand-holding as if they understand forgiveness, faith, trust, and love as companions.

I was in Evansville, Indiana the summer of 2014, at an antique show and flea market. I sat down on a bench and waited for my lady friend. I noticed an older couple near their 80s walking, holding hands and talking with laughter. The husband sat down beside me to wait on his wife as she went into the shelter to look over the tables.

This older man and I began to speak and I asked him a few questions. I asked, "What keeps you and your wife holding hands?" He replied, "Love, God, and the church." He had my attention with that answer. I asked him another question, "What keeps your love alive?" He replied, "Hard times and forgiving one another." I noticed that he was only answering with short answers, but he was on track with what I been teaching in the singles' ministry and these columns. He looked away and I had to ask him two more questions. I asked him how old he was and he pushed back his ball cap and replied, "86 years old." "Why do you hold hands with your wife", I asked? He replied, "It's a sign of love that has forgiven me all these years!"

His wife and my lady friend came back at the same time. I told him it was good talking to him; he laughed and told me to go to church. My lady friend asked me, "What was that about?" "Holding hands," I told her. On the first step from leaving that conversation, I placed my hand around my lady friend's hand and as we walked, I shared that conversation with her that I had with a man in love with his wife!

Why do people dating hold hands before they understand the true meaning of love? I have noticed in dating, people hold hands one day, and the next day, they seem to hate each other. People hold hands as if they have to, but where is their faith in this body language?

People have asked me about holding hands, and I ask them, "Why hold hands, if this is not the person you love and are willing to forgive?" They would look at me as if they never heard such! I find it amazing that people will hold hands with another person that they don't know. Holding hands is like a kiss in many ways. Why would you kiss or hold hands with a stranger?

I am one who believes in holding hands, but it has to be real! And a real relationship does not happen in a few weeks. **People think that they must kiss on the first date or hold hands within a few dates. Maybe it's people with expectations that may not be true.** Kissing on the first date is not needed. Men and boys, did you know that most girls and ladies would prefer not to be kissed on the first date?

We as single adults must place reality in our relationship development and with time the outcome will be truth. Truth brings a relationship into focus which takes some time. I think about marriages where the man and woman do not hold hands. They have lost the love of their friendship, haven't they? The next time you are out at one of the parks or an event, take the time to talk with an older person or couple and ask them why they hold hands. You will find it's not about action, but time that has kept their love alive!

That old man taught me a life lesson about holding hands with a lifetime of love, forgiveness, and understanding of companionship love that has stood the test of time!

UNDERSTANDING A RELATIONSHIP

Understanding a relationship should be a fun time. This is when you first meet, it's much like two strangers meeting, even if you think you know that person. We really do not know a person until we spend quality time with them. People say the craziest things, don't they? With that said, that's how to have a fun conversation in order to understand that person's behavior. This can lead to what a person needs to change if they want a real relationship.

I know a lot of people that speak with vanity. **IF YOU REALLY WANT A GREAT RELATIONSHIP A PERSON MUST STOP SPEAKING WITH VANITY.** Men and women, listen to what you say. Do not speak with uncertainties within your conversation, and in a relationship.

Be prepared to own what you say in the first few weeks of coming to know someone. If a person cannot own what they say, who are they trying to be? You do not need a fake acting person who talks like a clown do you? Do not have an alligator mouth and do not walk around with stupid written on your forehead. This would kill any chances for a relationship!

So, what does that new person talk about? It's OK if they talk about themselves or their job to a point. They may be building trust with you on that level. Here is what two people should talk about, what they know, what they desire, what they want and for most part a person's beliefs. Here's a great conversation starter, talk about each other's hobbies.

LEARN TO TAKE SPACE

This moves my pen to write this. **DO NOT SMOTHER A PERSON. Learn to take space in a new relationship, it's best not to see each other daily; remember it's good to have space.** You do not want to become a person that is addicted to having people in your life. **This type of addiction to people, will lead to smothering and possibly killing a relationship.** Learn this; it's OK to take space, it doesn't mean the other person doesn't care! This will also teach a person to control their jealous moods or behaviors.

PLEASE TALK ABOUT TAKING SPACE. It's wise not to ask that person what they did when space is taken. If that person wants to talk about the things they did while they were away, let them bring that conversation up. This is building trust and giving space. If you are having trouble with understanding space, talking about it will build trust and faith. **This is what friends should do, instead of stepping into the arena of jealousy.**

Should you date a person that wants to be with you all the time, this could be a sign of being immature or a person that may try to control you. Bring this last thought up in your conversation. Listen to what they are saying and question their thoughts if they sound immature or trying to control the relationship. Relationships will not grow if a person is not willing to mature.

You are going to find that there are adults that mature a little slower than the ordinary, within relationship development skills. Men and Women, must learn to grow in maturity. Yet, at the same time, do not be a parent to an adult! If I did not listen to a conversation in maturity from someone that I had an interest in, what would that person think? Here's a real question. **As a mature person, am I, worthy of being in a relationship with a mature person?**

A WORKING RELATIONSHIP

I always have been a busy person and by learning time management, I became better at working to have a greater relationship and social life. This is another life lesson for single adults and teens. Leave your work at work and learn to build a quality relationship with time!

ARE RELATIONSHIPS PERFECT? I think we all know the answer to that is, "No"! **The man and woman must work toward perfection in a long-term relationship and in a marriage.** Relationships are a lot of work. It's even more work to achieve real love and companionship in a marriage. **COUPLES MUST LEARN TO KEEP A RELATIONSHIP ALIVE OR IT WILL DIE.** The work you put toward changing yourself to have a greater relationship will be noticed by the other person in the relationship. This in turn will encourage that person to change as well.

This is worth noting: when the man and woman become and act like adults and stride toward learning maturity, I assure you, the relationship will grow and create a bond. The older the relationship is, the more we learn about ourselves and the other person; again, this is a labor of love! I will list eight areas in a relationship that people should take seriously and work through, if they want to have a great relationship and marriage.

1: Unique differences: **First, it is important to understand that each of us is unique.** The only person who can change their unacceptable ways is the same person who has it. We have to learn to change and it may take time and effort because change doesn't happen overnight. Our differences are part of our temperament. This is why a man and woman need to take a temperament test and couples need to understand the other person's temperament.

Ask a pastor or a counselor, about a temperament test or go online before you get engaged or married and take the temperament test. This will keep you from marrying a total stranger! If you think you know a person in less than 24 months, I will share with you, you really don't know them. To know someone takes a lifetime, doesn't it?

2: <u>Bad Habits:</u> These can involve both behavior and character issues. Bad habits at the beginning are related to behavior issues. The longer a person keeps a bad habit, the more likely it will become a part of their character. It is important for men and women to know the difference between a bad habit and a more serious character issue.

It takes less time to change a bad habit at the beginning than to allow it to become part of your character. Character changes take a lot longer. Adults should work on their bad habits without being told. **I would question the mental awareness, knowledge or character of any adult that has to be asked to work on or change their bad habits!** Single adults and teens should be aware of this: You do not need to have a relationship with someone that is not willing to change a bad habit! **Do you think a bad habit will cause a break up in a relationship? Sooner or later, their bad habits will condemn the relationship.**

3: <u>Time management:</u> This is a big issue for people and it should be addressed as the relationship grows. A person who is punctual (on time) will have a hard time understanding someone who isn't. A prompt person will not put up with excuses for long. Sooner or later, it will become an issue that both of you will have to face and work through. Single adults and young adults need to build understanding here.

BE ON TIME, ALL THE TIME!

4: <u>Finances:</u> I've seen people who have become married without the knowledge of each other's finances. This is a big mistake! This is an issue that should have been talked about before engagement and while your marriage counseling is going on. Things like payments, child support, bills, legal issues with debts and collections should be brought out into the open, as well as back taxes issues. A business that is owned by one person before marriage should remain in that person's possession. That business debts and assets should also be made available for discussion. No one in a relationship should hide his or her financial situation from the other.

5: <u>**Budgeting:**</u> If you're thinking about getting married. Think about this, create a checking account together. Sharing in the cost of a relationship while courting or engagement, shouldn't be too much to ask for? Sharing expenses will teach the man and woman that budgeting is a team responsibility. This helps a relationship in several ways. It allows couples to do more things. It teaches the two of you about budgeting. It helps to bond the couple in teamwork and provides understanding of each other's finances. In a marriage, even if you have a lot of money, it is important to accept financial responsibilities and budget together.

Just a note: If a man makes more money than a woman, it's OK. If a woman makes more money than a man, it's OK, too! It is OK to provide money in a relationship or marriage, provided each one understands the other's finances and the responsibility of a budget. Remember, in a marriage, a man and woman become one in unity, not a union.

6: <u>**Building and supporting hobbies:**</u> Hobbies are a plus for both the man and woman in a relationship and I encourage you to have a hobby. They can be different or they can be the same. Make sure your hobby fits within your budget. Here's a warning about hobbies – don't let your hobbies cross the line or take up more time and money than is healthy for the relationship. You don't want any hobby to break up a great relationship or marriage. Moderation is the key.

7: <u>**Cooking:**</u> Learn to cook together. Have cookouts for friends, family and coworkers. This is a lot of work, but the outcome is great and rewarding for you and your guests. Cooking also creates team skills and that increases relationship development. Another plus, is it gives you an opportunity to learn about healthy foods.

8: <u>**WORK TOWARD PERFECTION LIST.**</u> Perfection is an ongoing effort. I've written this topic to help you understand that your relationship needs two people who are willing to step up and work toward perfection. I've seen too many relationships and marriages that stop at the base of relationship building and never climb any higher into relationship development.

When a relationship stops growing it's because the couple have chosen to not walk together in companionship. Then the result is a dreadful relationship or marriage. The amount of love and quality of companionship, depends upon the effort that the couple makes in relationship development.

PART 4

A Few Things to Share

<u>RECEIVING AND GIVING A GIFT</u>

I never had a problem with giving a gift and thinking something was due to me. Yet, I have seen people who gave a gift and they expect something in return. That's not giving is it? It has been hard for me to learn to receive a gift from a woman / friend. Now I count it a blessing to receive a gift. Teenagers and single adults should have the understanding of receiving and giving a gift. Don't give a gift until you have come to know a person, please take some time in doing so. The money would be better used for your activities.

IF YOU CANNOT FREELY RECEIVE OR FREELY GIVE A GIFT, DO NOT RECEIVE OR GIVE A GIFT! Sometimes people give gifts so they can receive something, whether it's now or in the future. Giving a rose to a woman early in a relationship can be confusing. It may make a woman feel uncomfortable if she hasn't known you very long. She may think more of it than you meant. It doesn't mean the rose is a statement of love, it could be a person has taken some interest or a token of caring. **Men, if you give a rose (a gift), you should be clear about the meaning of the gift! Women if you receive a rose or gift, ask why, just to keep things in line and on the same page, so to speak.**

Birthday gifts are OK, but keep it small until the two of you have spent some time together. I would suggest a year. Taking someone out for dinner on their birthday is great and money well spent, and both can join in the fun of giving. There's a time and place for larger gifts and they should come after a year together, but remember the statement: freely you have received, freely you have given. **REAL GIFTS HAVE NO STRINGS ATTACHED.**

Commitment rings, should be based on how much time you have spent together. Wait until both of you show signs of genuine caring for each other. It is best to wait between six months to a year to give this kind of ring, or when a man and woman are in courtship. **This is not a pre-engagement ring.**

Pre-engagement rings: Are acceptable after a year or so. Try to buy one from a store that will let you trade it in for an engagement ring. You're trying to invest in a lifetime, so go slow with the rings. Parents and Pastors like it when couples share with them that they are pre-engaged. **THIS SHOWS SIGNS OF BUILDING MATURITY IN A RELATIONSHIP.**

Note: all rings have a marked-up price of 50% to 125%, I've seen people who bought rings for a few thousand dollars, just to find out their ring had little value, (just a few hundred dollars). Do not allow a jewelry store to take advantage of you and your relationship. Have them appraise the ring you are looking to buy and see if they will tell you the truth! Ask when this ring is going to go on sale. The real value of a ring is that it's a gift to show a sign of commitment. (Appraiser: "to value", is one who determines the fair market value of property, real or personal.) *Even when a ring is on sale, there may still be a 35 to 50 percent mark-up on a ring.*

Engagement rings: AS A MAN, PARENT AND A MATURE ADULT, I STRONGLY ADVISE THAT YOU DO NOT BUY ONE UNTIL BOTH OF YOU AGREE ON THIS. This will save you time and money. If one of you is not ready to be engaged, do not become offended or upset. It may just mean that the hesitant one needs a little more time to think it over, and of course, I say take all the time you need! **Asking to be engaged is a mature thing to do before you buy a ring, please learn this.** Do not catch someone off guard, this can be embarrassing. Talk about engagement is what adults should do anyway. This will save the embarrassment.

A relationship takes time to build. Before you consider becoming engaged, you should have been in a 6 to 12-month courtship, and engagements should last between six months to a year or more before you marry. Solid marriages take time to build.

I hope you understand more clearly about gifts. Not all gifts are given with love. Just take your time and remember that whether you are giving or receiving a gift, it must be for all the right reasons. This is good and practical information for everyone!

<u>NEVER HAVE ANOTHER BROKEN HEART</u>

I am not the first person to have a broken heart or relationship issues that led me into depression from a lack of knowledge. **<u>PLEASE TAKE THIS TOPIC SERIOUSLY.</u>** I ask you as a reader to learn this step of life management skills, as I had to learn, "**NEVER HAVE ANOTHER BROKEN HEART**"!

I have learned that there has been a lot of suicide due to broken relationships. It can be one or a few broken relationships that can cause a person to think low of themselves. **<u>SINGLE ADULTS AND TEENS, BREAKUPS ARE A FACT THAT TWO PEOPLE CAN NOT MAKE THE RELATIONSHIP WORK. THIS SHOULD BE UNDERSTOOD AS A BLESSING!</u>** This is why we should build friendship first. Remain friends, even if the relationship doesn't work. This may save a person from depression. Think about this, you have to be the right person for the right relationship!

How many times have you seen a relationship that has broken apart and then observed one, or even both of the individuals dwelling in depression? Of course, there may be sadness at the beginning of a breakup, people choose how they are going to react with self-pity or confusion. I had a pastor friend tell me one day, that there comes a point in depression when a person chooses to stay in that condition of depression. At that point, it can be called selfishness. **(Note: this is not clinical depression I am talking about!)** I agree with him because I experienced depression when a few of my relationships ended.

I chose to stay depressed; because it was like hanging onto my part of the relationship and that is not reality! It was a state of confusion that soon became selfishness! *After a breakup in a relationship, there is nothing to hang onto, other than to remain friendly!* Please understand this in your thoughts and heart!

Vain imagination can take over a person's depression. Dwelling on past issues can keep a person on the path of depression! **We as a person, are** not meant to live in a depressed state of mind or attitude. Another pastor shared with me the statement that we should live by: "**NEVER LOVE ANYONE MORE THAN GOD!**"

DO PEOPLE HAVE A RIGHT TO CHOOSE WITH WHOM THEY WANT TO HAVE A RELATIONSHIP WITH? People should keep their eyes and heart focused on who they can be for that right person and that special someone. We will use our free will to choose the right person from within our own wisdom, then our choice's may and can be blessed! Seek the right person to have a great relationship with and not another broken relationship!

So, why have mental stress or depression after a break up? You only need that one right person to build a relationship with and to marry. If love seems to die, it may have never had a real cause to live or to take root. Therefore, there is no one to blame, is this not a true statement?

PART 5

Cohabitation Knowledge

I believe in marriage and I know people live together for many reasons. Yet cohabitation was one of my biggest failures in trying to have a relationship that left two people hurt and confused.

Living with someone outside of marriage is one of the biggest mistakes that I have made! It will hurt both the man and woman when they realize this is not going to work! This isn't about judging. It's about the truth and the harm it causes. I will be writing from experience, studies, research, education, writings and involvement in singles' ministries on this issue of cohabitation. I'll share with you some facts and percentages (*some of these facts and percentages are my opinions*). As you read this topic, open your heart and mind to these facts that I have learned and experienced. **Please, this is not to offend anyone; you are going to read what I have come to learn.**

The beginning of a friendship or relationship is always fun and full of excitement. I am sure you know this. The truth or seeking the truth in a relationship has a way of bringing that newness and fun to a reality, or to say, the understanding of a relationship. Subsequently, at that point, the question comes up about whether the relationship has a chance of working out or not. More often, this is done while the man and woman are in a cohabitating lifestyle.

The first-time marriage, has a 50 percent chance of lasting a lifetime. Cohabitation (living together) has a 25 percent chance of lasting a lifetime. **When a person says they love someone enough to live with them, which of the two situations (marriage or cohabitation) would you as a person** want as a lifelong relationship? What are your thoughts about living together versus marriage?

Think for a minute about what you know about this subject of cohabitation. Consider seriously about what it would be like to live with someone that you are not married to. I want you to understand that cohabitation is living within mistakes and sin if you are having sex. Cohabitation does not build companionship love, which only happens after marriage?

CAN I HAVE YOUR ATTENTION? More than 60 to 65 percent of the single adults in America are living together. COHABITATION HAS BECOME MORE HARMFUL TO FAMILIES THAN DIVORCE, AND IT CAN, AND HAS, DISPLACED MARRIAGES. Cohabitation has a very high rate of separation, more so, than divorce.

I have called this COHABITATION DIVORCE"! Cohabitation divorce has a 30 percent higher failure rate than first-time marriages in America. While the first-time marriage, in America, has a divorce rate around 50 percent, the first-time *cohabitation divorce* rate is 70 or 80 percent. What causes these failures? Once again, this is my opinion, I have learned.

1: The man and woman have left the principle of marriage out of their relationship development. Where is the foundation of faith in cohabitation! In order to have the companionship love that comes through marriage, one must be married and work toward the truth of a real companionship relation. This takes a few years to understand and work toward. Can this happen with cohabitation? Yes, but more than likely it will never reach this position. This is due to the man and woman not acting like husband and wife.

The man or woman in cohabitation will learn that there was no real love in this type of relationship, just fornication and wishful thinking! Most couples living together outside marriage will not marry and will go through what I have called, "THE COHABITATION DIVORCE."

2: The man and woman have moved into an UNSTABLE RELATIONSHIP built on expectation and imagination, and we call this cohabitation! It starts with those three words, "I love you," and then comes the sexual part of the relationship that is built on lust. Real, lifelong relationships are not built on lust or sex!

When a man and woman have known each other only for a short time and decide to move in together for reasons of thinking they love each other and having sex, they have skipped the very important stage of building friendship first in their relationship. **Here is a real question that you will have to answer: How can a person love someone who is not a friend?** You may be thinking that you two are friends. But here is another question that this couple will have to answer: <u>**IF SOMEONE PULLS YOU DOWN INTO LUST OR JUST USING YOU FOR SEX AND A PLACE TO STAY, ARE THEY REALLY BEING A FRIEND?**</u> Lust does not last long, much less a lifetime, does it?

People in cohabitation typically will split up and end the relationship within 2 to 24 months. Is the road to cohabitation a dead-end road? Here are the losses that can occur in this type of relationship. You will gain a broken heart, guilt, shame, may end up hating the other person that you thought you loved, embarrassment and the painful awareness that you have been living within a real mistake. You may lose your personal property, a place to live, your self-respect, and your self-confidence. All of this, just because people have refused to live the right way.

3: **Have men and women confused union with unity?** Do people know the difference? **When they cohabitate, or "SHACK UP," is it a UNION or UNITY?** Think for a moment before you answer that question. Is marriage a union or unity? Here is my opinion, unity comes from marriage only! Read the book of Genesis for more information on this.

Unity does not have by-laws; only the blessings of a covenant. Marriage brings two people together in unity. Does cohabitation bring unity? If you said "No", you're right!

When a man and a woman are married and they have a home, all that they have is owned by the two of them as if it were owned by one, through unity.

Now let's look at cohabitation. Is it a union or unity? It has to be one of the two. I looked for the word *union* in my Bible and I could not find this word union and I do not think it is in the Bible! The word *unity* is in the Bible. I believe that unity is the Christian or greater foundation for marriage. Union is a worldly or business arrangement.

<u>Men and women, who live together, make their own rules.</u> **There is no covenant in cohabitation, it's just man-made and is mixed with by-laws!** Why do you think people cohabitate instead of marrying? Perhaps they skipped the relationship development time frame and jumped off of lover's leap.

HOW FAR WILL TWO PEOPLE FALL FROM LOVERS LEAP, BEFORE THEY CRASH? Imagine, consider, and think before you jump off of Lover's Leap; there is going to be a lot of pain. When the couple hits the ground, more than likely the relationship will die!

Here is a sampling of issues that a man and a woman will have to live by in cohabitation. **They live in a house that is not a home!** If an unmarried person owns a home, will they willingly give it to the other person in the relationship? Of course not! When you move in with someone, what is theirs is not yours and what is yours is not theirs. That is not oneness, is it? In a marriage there should be only one check-book (not counting businesses) for paying household bills. When you live together with someone, all things, including money, are separate – either yours or theirs. That is not the case in a real marriage. Couples should talk about and share the budget / payments of the needed bills.

There will be other rules usually made by the people who move in with each other as cohabitants. These are man-made rules, and that may or will leave love out of the rulings. Man-made rules or by-laws have a bottom line that state, *"It's my way or the highway."* Rules that aren't made within love, set up this false relationship for failure!

Cohabitation is like playing a game; three strikes and you're out! In a marriage, the man and woman work through their unique differences and temperaments with understanding. Why, because they are committed to support the unity of marriage! A person may not see this in a cohabitation lifestyle. Eighty percent of people who live together are in bondage by selfishness from the other person, and they find themselves being treated like a servant. *Are people living together without any real commitment?*

Imagine the effects of having a child while cohabitating with someone. **<u>WHAT SECURITY DOES THAT CHILD HAVE WITH UNMARRIED PARENTS?</u>** What security is there for a child brought into cohabitation from a previously broken home? These children live with anxiety and embarrassment because their parents are not married.

Children who live within cohabitation go to school and church where they hear other children and people state, that people who live together should be married. **Cohabitation not only confuses the adults it also confuses the children as well.** Through cohabitation the child is raised within a union of by-laws that is not based on the structure of love as a family!

What will children think of their parents for putting them in the position of being ashamed of the lifestyle their parents have chosen? How will cohabitating parents explain that to their children? Will people of cohabitation say, "I did not care, I had no knowledge, or I was too self-seeking and immature to do the right thing?" **Can you honestly expect children to ever have real respect for those answers?**

Cohabitating parents are sacrificing their child's sense of family security and setting children up for failure, not to mention setting an example that they may follow. That is what is being done today in America and around the world, and we think cohabitation is OK! Is that what we want for our children? We have already seen what happens to young adults that do not live in a covenant family or without a father or mother figure.

Adults can walk away from cohabitation a lot easier than they can in a marriage. There is something about marriage that tends to keep people married. I think it's the family structure that comes from the covenant of marriage.

The men and women living together will more than likely skip any counseling from a counselor or minister on marriage! That in itself is a major mistake. Marriage counseling is truly important. Most people are blindsided when they get married because they do not have the facts of marriage. **Marriage is a true labor of love. There might not be a labor of love in cohabitation!**

If you're going to live together, you must learn to forgive. To understand forgiveness, you need the knowledge and the understanding of life skills, people skills and relationship skills. The Bible offers many life lessons and great moral values within its writings. How will you learn to forgive the one you're living with, without the value of knowledge? It's true that love forgives all sin and mistakes, but just like forgiving, most people do not understand love either.

IF YOU'RE THINKING THIS IS JUST MY OPINION, YOU'RE RIGHT! So now I ask you, what is your opinion about cohabitation?

PART 6

Effects of How We Care

I CARE, AND I DON'T CARE. These two cares are part of one's behavior and character. If someone cannot change their behavior or character, they will live a life of I don't care and say the verbal statement of, "I do not care", a lot! What's sad is that they mean or believe that statement.

Single adults and teenagers alike have real issues with the two cares of life. It's important to know if you care or not. Eventually everyone must come to understand how they truly feel. Do you know if you care or not? *To do extremely well in relationship development, you must learn to care!* This is part of good people skills, isn't it? Stay away from people who say they don't care.

When I don't care is said! Perhaps that person has given up. Maybe they do not have enough encouragement to tackle the issues of life or things that matter. Maybe it's their education level or lack of understanding. It can also have something to do with one's maturity level. Whatever the reason is, it comes from behavior or character, or both.

What do you really mean when you say "I don't care"? Do you use body language when you say it? **IF YOU KNOW SOMETHING ABOUT AN ISSUE YOU CAN'T REALLY SAY, "I DON'T CARE."** You probably are being unconcerned or negative. Maybe you're trying to get your way. Maybe you're tired and you're allowing the I don't care, to control your mind.

When it comes to relationship development, why would you date/ court or even marry a person who hides behind the statement of, "I don't care"? **There can be no, "I don't care" in relationship development if** the relationship is to grow. You cannot build a relationship with someone who states "I do not care"!

"I CARE", comes from the heart and mind of a person, and from one who has searched for a better lifestyle! One's lifestyle is based on development in maturity, knowledge and wisdom, and it should be! The majority of the time, when a person states, "I don't care", it comes from a person's lack of maturity or wisdom. Wisdom is always knowledge that works for and towards a better future!

Now the question remains, are you a person that cares or are you a person who doesn't care? I have lived both lifestyles of the two cares; life became better for me when I understood to care for myself and others! What would happen if you cared?

WHEN WE SAY, I LOVE YOU

When we say I love you in a new relationship, what are we really saying? People say these three words so effortlessly, but we think they really mean what they say. It can be said with the right intentions, but for the wrong reasons. Love takes time to build. The proof of that is; people need to build trust and friendship before love can grow! They may love the activity level of a new relationship, and be so excited and energetic, that they forget about whom they are really having a relationship with. Just because we can be inspired by someone, doesn't mean love will grow. Love is a two-sided relationship.

It can take men about four to six months to realize they love someone, and most men are like me; they need to build trust. Women can grow in love, or have the emotion of love, sooner than men. Here is a little scenario; people who say I love you within two weeks or so, may be a person that is addicted to having people in their life! I've had this happen to me. If a man is hanging on to a relationship more than four to six months, he is building trust and a commitment. It is hard for men, to say "I love you", especially when they realize they really are in love.

A man will listen to a woman say, "I love you," and not be moved in the way a woman wants him to move emotionally. It takes time for a man to understand his behavior of love. I want to point this out about men, for the most, men are not friend based and perhaps men don't understand friendship from not trusting. THIS BRINGS ME TO SAY, MEN HAVE

TO BE TAUGHT HOW, AND WHAT IS LOVE, MORE THAN A WOMAN! That was a life skill statement wasn't it?

From my point of view, if women say they are in love, men, listen to what they are saying. If you have an interest at this point, share with that lady that you have a greater interest in her and allow time to build a loving relationship. I have done this. **I always work toward building trust and friendship in a relationship first.** Men and women need to learn to take their time, and build a relationship to establish a real foundation for friendship and love. This foundation for a relationship will become a blessing!

If the man or woman states to the other person, that their feelings are headed toward love, and the other person leaves the relationship, then they were not interested in having a long-term relationship or a loving relationship with that person. **I want to be clear here. There is no one to blame.** If a person stays with the other person after they have stated that their feelings are headed toward love, they need to give the other person time to realize if they want to have a deeper relationship too. The longer you build trust and friendship, the truth will come out. As a man, this is how I have seen myself growing in love.

I'm so careful in using these three words, "I love you". I do not allow myself to feed off someone's behavior. As a man, I am more action minded and I hold back my emotions. I also stay in control of my expectations and imagination. I have had a few ladies tell me they love me, only to find out they were just misusing these words. Perhaps ladies this has happened to you as well. **You do not need to ask someone if they like you.** *It will show!* **DO NOT SAY, "I LOVE YOU", UNTIL LOVE HAS A REAL MEANING!**

YOUR LOVE ON TRIAL

This thought of having your love on trial came to me one day. I've had a lot of friends enjoy this writing. As you read this allow the theater of your mind to work; *YOU ARE ON TRIAL FOR LOVE*!

You have been asked to come to a court of law to prove your love that you have claimed. You're in love with this other person in your relationship and you have to represent yourself. As you read, **"YOU ARE ON TRIAL FOR LOVE,"** have a mental image of a courtroom setting. The judge happens to be the person you say you love. The jury is made up of people from your past relationships.

You are walking into the courtroom. Your friends, people from your church, co-worker, your ex's, and a few of your family members, are sitting in this courtroom to give you support; but they are looking at you with suspicion. Now, as you walk to your seat, you begin to wonder about yourself and the outcome of this trial. You take your seat. It's only you and a glass of water that will separate you from the jury and the judge. You are hearing a few comments in the background.

Out walks the people who make up the jury (all of your ex's), and they all look at you, one at a time. They are just as dumbfounded as you are. There is a chill in this courtroom as you wait. The judge walks out to take a seat, smiles, and wonders what you are going to say. Now, remember, it's up to the jury to make the decision, if you are telling the truth.

The judge reads why you're here, and then reads a statement that you must answer. The judge has asked you to prove that you love this person in your relationship. You must convince this jury and the judge by writing out a detailed outline of facts and reasons why you have a real love for the other person involved. You have 30 minutes. You are given a pen and pad and you begin to write your testimony. Thirty minutes have passed.

The judge has just walked back into the courtroom. Everyone has taken their seat. The judge has given you the allowed time. It's time to hand over the facts and your written testimony. The judge has asked that you read your statement to the jury and court. You complete your statement. Now you wonder how the jury and judge took it.

Then a man walks into the courtroom. He begins to speak with wisdom, to inform the court and you what real love is! The court and you sit back to listen not knowing what to expect.

There is a sound of thunder as this strange man begins to speak. "Real relationships need real commitments of love, compassion, forgiveness, understanding of people and life skills, and most of all friendship. You will need to renew your love every day, if you wish to have love for life. If love is going to stand the test of time, freely give and freely receive!"

What are your facts and reasons why you have a real love for the other person involved?

PART 7

Thoughts of Marriage

I was one that did not listen to my marriage counseling and did not have a good understanding of counseling from my self-made, lack of knowledge. **Counseling is not saying a person is crazy or they have a mental disorder, it is a tool to help you in life skills!** I had to learn that from my school of hard knocks. Please do not get married until you have had at least six months of marriage counseling! This will keep you from marrying a total stranger. This should help couples learn that they do not know everything about relationships and marriage.

Throughout this book I have been sharing a lot about relationship development. *Relationships are a lot of work and keeping a marriage healthy is a lot more work?* I want you and everyone to know that before you get married you still have the right to end the relationship, even while you are engaged. **THIS IS THE TIME TO THINK SERIOUSLY ABOUT YOURSELF AND THE OTHER PERSON.** Think about what you have read in this book and what you should have learned in marriage counseling. I want to emphasize the importance of marriage counseling. It is in the best interest of both the man and woman who are considering marriage. **AM I TRYING TO TALK YOU OUT OF MARRIAGE? NO, I AM TRYING TO STOP ANOTHER DIVORCE!**

Most people will tell you that the first three to six months of marriage is great, before the "feel good stage" or passion wears off, so to speak. During this time, the couple is living off the excitement of the new marriage. Soon, the reality of day-to-day issues with another person sets in. This is where your people skills will come into play and should be

46

understood; please do not forget this! If you marry a person without people skills, what type of person have you married?

ONCE MARRIED, YOU CANNOT PUT THE ANIMAL BACK IN THE CAGE, CAN YOU? We all have been told throughout life that you really don't know a person. You will realize the meaning of that statement after the first six months of marriage. Laugh now, but remember this next statement; my hope is that you do not marry a stranger!

I did not write that to put fear into your marriage. We must have the understanding that there is going to be a lot of work toward companionship in your marriage. **This is called, the <u>LABOR OF LOVE IN MARRIAGE</u> and it should be called that! MARRIAGE IS A LABOR OF LOVE!** The problems at this labor of love stage, must be addressed and worked out with love from both the man and woman. We can start with the hidden issues.

Men, women are not your mother! Women, men are not your dad! This is one, if not the greatest, area of change. Both husband and wife need to learn to cook, clean the house, do laundry, do yard work, pay bills together, shop together and so on. **This helps with time management, budgeting and cooperation.** What if one of the spouses is a stay at home person or works from home. Here's the great news: **it is the same, working together is bonding.**

Bonding creates a team effect and keeps the two of you working in unity. Without unity, this stage of the marriage will not be fun. If you can't work as a team on all the things I mentioned above, then one, if not both of you, will wish you had not married in the first place. It is important when working together as spouses, not to have unrealistic expectations. Remember it takes time to learn. This is a relationship skill that needs to be understood.

Cooking, what to buy at the grocery, the varieties of healthy foods and your spouse's preferences in foods, are areas that can become big issues just as much as cleaning up after yourself! If spouses would learn to resolve these issues that I mention, the other part of working together would come a lot easier. Just like building a relationship of courting and engagement, it takes time to build a good team that works with unity within a marriage.

<u>**ANOTHER BIG ISSUE IS PERSONAL HYGIENE**</u>: Men, I been told by women who are married that men need to know that women do not like to be physical, with a man, if they are not keeping themselves clean. I want to add a stern statement. I have been an Army contractor and had up to fifty men, working under me in Iraq. *In my lifetime of working, the only*

people I had to talk to about their personal hygiene, were men. As adults, take a bath or shower before you go to bed or have a physical activity with a woman. **Men do you know, if you do not keep yourself clean, women can become infected by your uncleanness?** Is this enough said?

I suggest that you wait a year and a half to two years before having that first child. This will allow your marriage some time to mature! Children are a lot of work and effort. They cost a lot and take up a lot of time. **Children will add to the labor of love; you need to know this!**

If you married someone who already has a child or children, there will be even more work to do and you will face a lot more emotions. Be aware, building a strong family unit within a blended family, requires a lot more work. Don't forget that you will have to put up with that child's father or mother, if they are still around. A reminder, that last statement is an issue that should have been discussed in your marriage counseling. I'd like to include here a column I wrote about arguments. You will have them, so please read on.

ARGUMENTS

I am going to deal with arguments from a relationship point of view. I've had a few arguments and I have a few more to come. Arguing can be both good and bad in a relationship. If we could keep arguments from leading to bad behaviors, this would be healthy for the relationship. Couples need to stick to the details of the issue at hand while in an argument. We all have good and bad days and this should be recognized. What will it gain if a person keeps arguing? Life and relationships are already complicated. Why would anyone want to add to this?

I want you to note something – it's OK to have a point of view, because we all have a free will. Sometimes the issue we argue about is not right or wrong, it is just a point of view. Some people argue to have control. That is misleading and will unbalance or destroy a relationship and marriage.

If we are going to have a great relationship, we must learn to understand another person's point of view. No two people are alike. Men and women have their unique differences and this makes up life and is a part of all relationships!

<u>Argue</u>: to exchange views about something to arrive at the truth, or convince others, to contend in words, to give evidence of or serve as ground

for a valid or reasonable inference, and to uphold as true, right and proper, or acceptable often in the face of challenge or indifference.

If we argue, we must learn how to arrive at the truth!
If we argue without peace, no one will listen!

"The truth shall set you free." In order to be set free, you must have peace. The truth will either set you free, or cause you to have problems with the way you think! Listening and arguing is like a two-sided coin, you must have both. In order to arrive at the truth, we must listen to the argument. When one argues without a listener, we have no foundation for the truth to stand on. The ear that hears the rebukes of life will abide among the wise. He who disregards instruction despises his own soul, but he who heeds to rebuke may get understanding.

If we become offended with someone's argument, we must consider what the argument is about. When something needs to be confronted, or when something needs to be changed, the truth needs to be found. Keep in mind we all must learn to forgive each other.

What good is an argument, if we haven't learned how to argue? Arguing is not speaking loudly to each other. **If you have to scream at one another, this is not an argument. It is only discord and it will keep you from the truth and pull away at the foundation of any relationship and marriage. The truth must do two things before it can set you free. It has to inform you and change you!**

I want to emphasize that life and relationships are not about winning every argument. We must allow people to change themselves. If you cannot get along, just move on. This would be a blessing anyway! If you are married and argue all the time, only two things will come out of this type of relationship and that is living in hell and soon the divorce will come! So, before you get married, to save a marriage or relationship, **COUPLES WILL HAVE TO LEARN HOW TO ARGUE WITH LOVE! If you plan to marry, can you honestly say you can problem solve issues? Marriage is not and should not be one-sided, if so, love will die. Then the couple will live with a stranger and have an unhappy marriage!**

I HAVE A VERY STRONG SUGGESTION. I want everyone that's going to or is married to follow up on their marriage counseling! Do this after one year of marriage and every two years thereafter, from the start of your marriage! Go to the same pastor or counselor that worked with you before, if possible. If not, talk with a <u>Pastor</u> or <u>marriage counselor</u>.

Did you say, **"WHY"**? I'm glad you asked. **It's to save and place your marriage on the right road for life, and to teach both of you to stay committed!** Now here are some **"What-If"**? What if, one of the spouses has brought up issues that have not been resolved? What if, unforgiving has set in or someone has a bad habit they choose not to change? **What if, there is some type of mental nonsense going on between the two of you that needs to be resolved? THERE IS A LOT OF WHAT-IF, IN THE FIRST FEW YEARS OF MARRIAGE!**

I believe if couples would go back after one year of marriage, for **counseling and have a "check-up," their marriage could stand the test of time.** I strongly recommend this "one-year check-up" and counseling should become a part of every marriage!

PART 8

Engagement

PRE-ENGAGEMENT

PRE-ENGAGEMENT: This subject will help a man and woman by giving them something to think about before stepping into engagement. No rings are needed at this point. A commitment ring or friendship ring is OK. Here are my suggestions about pre-engagement. **<u>Consider pre-engagement after six months of dating!</u>** Pre-engagement should last six months as well.

    1: You should have been dating or courting for at least six months or more. During this time, the man and woman should have spent time building trust, truth, faith and friendship. It usually takes around a year of spending time together to develop trust and to understand the truth of any relationship! Investing time in the relationship allows the man and woman to become friends and eventually best friends. You need a best friend to go the distance in a long-term relationship and marriage. **I believe that parents and pastors should strongly recommend pre-engagement before engagement.** If you are trying to spend a lifetime together, a few more months wouldn't hurt. Besides, this may prevent a divorce and we will talk about divorce later in this book.

    2: Learn about your temperament so you can learn about who you are; this will give a person more respect for the other person. You can go online and take a temperament test. I also suggest, giving the temperament test results to your counselor and allow him to talk to you about your temperament, behaviors and character. This is a good time to confess whatever is needed and allow the gift of repenting to heal your past. This process will give you a greater future.

3: Do not start having sex. If you are having sex, just stop; this will give you a clearer vision of the relationship! You do not need to enter your marriage, with sin or lust attached to your relationship.

4: I would recommend spending more time with each other. This will give you both a chance to search for the truth in yourself and the relationship. Marriage is for a lifetime, and if you learn to spend time together while pre-engaged, it would be time well spent.

5: If possible, this is also a time to talk with each other's parents and children. It is a time to share with them that the two of you are thinking about marriage. You should let them know if you plan to marry. When you involve the parents, you're asking for and seeking their support. The man and woman both will need their support! Pre-engagement is similar to courtship, yet it is a deeper relationship that moves the man and woman to engagement.

ENGAGEMENT

<u>I strongly suggest that before you consider engagement you should spend at least 12 to 18 months dating or courting with pre-engagement.</u> Engagement should be six months or longer! This will allow a person to spend enough time with the other person that brings forth important truths about each other. This is the beginning of a mature relationship and there should be enough trust in the relationship now for you to make the decision, if this is the person you want to spend a lifetime with.

This book teaches you about relationship development and has made you more aware and mature in having a relationship! I want you to have the understanding of this next statement. **"Men and women both are looking for a mature person to have a relationship with, in order to build a great marriage!"**

THE ENGAGEMENT RING: It is only customary to consider an engagement ring. It doesn't mean you need or must have an engagement ring, to be engaged. The engagement ring is used as a token of your commitment before marriage, but it is still not a wedding ring. Since engagement rings are expensive, it would be a good idea to look into the cost, and remember your budget. Not everyone can afford engagement rings, and that's all right. (*I like to think that both the man and woman should pick out the rings together. I know the woman would want this. Besides, it is a gift for the man and woman!*) Some people don't use engagement rings or a wedding band, this needs to be understood as well.

What is very important at this point is counseling. Counseling should last for six months and courting for at least 12 to 18 months. This allows the man and woman time to adjust their temperament, behaviors, character, and any bad habits. These are changes that need to be made for the sake of the relationship and marriage.

You do not want to marry a total stranger, do you? It takes a long time to know someone. Ask your marriage counselor, pastor, and most of all, your parents if marriage is right for you. <u>SEEK THIS ADVICE! If you do not, you may very well marry a stranger!</u> If a person does not face the truth, they may be the stranger!

Too many people marry couples, who have not spent enough time together and have not had any marriage counseling. **If you marry too quickly you will more than likely make the statement that so many married couples have, <u>"I MARRIED A STRANGER."</u>** While there is humor in the statement there is also truth! When you marry a stranger, a few things are likely to happen.

<u>A WORKING MARRIAGE / COUNSELING</u>

1: You're going to have to work through stage one of your marriage. This is called understanding the stranger you married. Remember the words, "I love you." This will reinforce your marriage as it turns into a labor of love! *I want to be really clear here, people are going to marry a stranger, no matter how long you have known a person!*

2: **Marriage counseling should also be considered after the first year of marriage! No exceptions on this, this could save a lot of marriages!** *Pastors and counselors, you need to be aware of this and try to enforce this!* <u>I also believe it would be a great idea to have marriage counseling meetings after one or two years of married!</u> *You say this cost money and I say it's a lot cheaper than a divorce!* If you do not think this is a good investment for your marriage, then what are you investing in? Men, women would love for you to seek marriage counseling, there is more nonsense in marriage then one would believe. Men if you love your wife, take this as great advice!

3: **A lot of pastors do not have knowledge in relationship development, temperament testing, and marriage counseling.** Selecting a good marriage counselor is a must! I did not have a good marriage counselor! This caused me to have the effects of, (*I married a stranger*), then the divorce happened within a few years. Counseling will make you think about what you want out of marriage and what will occur during marriage.

If a couple, are mindset on getting married, I suggest you find someone that does a six months counseling program! Too many times pastors and people, have married couples that they do not know. Here is what you can hear: "I married them," and in a few months or a few years, they will hear that the couple they married have divorced. God forbid that you seek to get a divorce. Divorce takes away from the labor of love which produces companionship within a marriage! Fight the good fight of faith!

Here is what is sad, 50 percent or more of people and pastors that marry a man or woman, do not have this understanding or education of marriage counseling! People and pastors should not marry total strangers! I know people and pastors that have married a man and woman within two weeks, or less than six months of knowing each other. I think these people and pastors should become educated! Would this help prevent a divorce and lower the divorce rate?

PRENUPTIAL AGREEMENT

I will keep this next subject short as I can. Please keep this in mind as you read, **THIS IS NOT ANY FORM OF LEGAL ADVICE!** It is a subject that has been brought up at the singles' ministry programs I had, and one-on-one conversations with single adults. I feel it needs to be addressed.

Now, let's look at what exactly this agreement is about. This may well be the first time you have thought about a prenuptial agreement, so I want you to be open-minded here. Some of you have considered this subject before, so, take note of this information.

First is fairness! Remember you are marrying someone who has become your best friend! Find an attorney that will help the two of you to focus on the fairness of a prenuptial agreement. I know that you can review a free prenuptial agreement on the Internet. Notice, I said to review. **DO NOT**

SIGN A PRENUPTIAL AGREEMENT WITHOUT THE ADVICE OF AN ATTORNEY! We all have that last statement understood, right?

When considering an attorney, look for one that would serve the best interest of both the man and woman. Once again, the goal is fairness. It's alright to use one lawyer and it's alright to use two. It depends on the available income and or the business structure of the two people involved.

There are a lot of things to consider at this point and it's important that you give these matters enough attention before you contact an attorney. In keeping it short, here's a list of things I suggest you think over.

Do a background check on one another. The man and woman wish to enter into a prenuptial agreement for status, ownership and division of property between them, including future property owned, or to be acquired by either or both of them. The parties further wish to affix their respective rights and liabilities that may result from this relationship. The parties recognize the possibility of unhappy differences that may arise between them. Parties acknowledge that they have been provided with a reasonable period of time to review this agreement. Parties acknowledge that they have had the opportunity to retain their own lawyer and received legal advice regarding the terms of this agreement. Parties have disclosed all assets and liabilities that each one has. Parties acknowledge that this agreement will continue upon termination of marriage whether by death, divorce, or otherwise.

Here are the considerations: Property, Debts, Matrimonial property release, Dower curtesy and homestead release, Support, Estate and testamentary disposition, Severability, Intention of parties, Duty of good faith, Further documentation, Title/Heading, Increment, Governing Law, Termination or amendment.

These considerations are real and become serious issues at the end of a marriage, whether by death divorce or otherwise. You or your heirs, executors, administrators, and assigns could and may have legal issues with a prenuptial agreement. This is costly in terms of time and money.

Now it is time for **my reflection** on the matter of prenuptial agreements. There are pastors that agree and pastors that don't agree with prenuptial agreements. A couple, especially a Christian couple who desire to unite in marriage, should seek first to have a Godly marriage. A prenuptial agreement might be needed *for the right reasons* but it is not to be used as a way of escaping a marriage if one or both are not satisfied. It is wrong to use a prenuptial agreement as an escape if the marriage doesn't work out and the couple thinks divorce will be simpler. It is wrong to use any legal instrument that displace the plans for a covenant of marriage.

A prenuptial agreement is not needed for a first-time marriage unless there is a large amount of wealth and or business assets. A prenuptial agreement is a valid consideration for a second marriage, with or without children, but as I stressed above, put a covenant of marriage first.

What is a COVENANT? Most people believe it's a marriage made between God and the man and woman, not men and their many laws. Bring this up in your marriage counseling.

If you're waiting for my opinion, here it goes: Any time mankind changes the plans that are good, he instills a spirit of confusion. If you think divorce is hard, try a divorce with a prenuptial agreement. The lawyers are the only ones that come out with a smile and a paycheck!

PART 9

Reality of A Divorce

My divorce left me feeling hopeless, full of hate, bitterness and irritation. Not counting being broken from having to find a place to live, child support and day care. The hatefulness that I shared with my ex-wife showed how immature a man or a person can become after a divorce. **I should have received counseling over my divorce and I think most people should!** Knowledge of divorce, may help to stop another divorce. I wish I could have read a book like this, before I married. **Please tell your friends and love one's about this book!**

It's easy to explain love at first sight – that's expectation and imagination! Did you know that 51 percent of adults believe in love at first sight, I heard that on a radio talk show one day while working? If love at first sight is a true statement, why didn't they get married or stay married? How do we explain love after two people have been married to each other for years? How have they kept their love and marriage alive? **Success in marriage does not come by finding the right person. it comes from being the right person!** It is not the marriage that fails. It is the people in the marriage that fail to keep real love in the relationship alive! What is real love? It's a working love that is full of commitment and understanding. It's a love of hope and faith! It's a love that forgives. **THIS IS WHAT I CALL, "THE LABOR OF LOVE"!**

No man or woman can simply promise to keep a marriage together without real companionship and love based on unity. No one's wisdom, knowledge or wealth can make a marriage successful. Marriage is kept together by love that is real and full of friendship and understanding the strategy for marriage! **In this modern age, very few couples will survive a marriage without faith.**

The U.S. Census Bureau in 1900 reported the rate of divorce was about 1 in every 100. During the Great Depression in the 1930s, the divorce rate was 5 in every 100 marriages. During World War II, the divorce rate continued to increase to 11 in 100 marriages. In the 1970s, **"NO FAULT DIVORCE"** came along. It is from that time until now that divorce rates have increased to the estimation that 1 out of 2 marriages will fail. That's 50 percent! Before the **"NO FAULT DIVORCE,"** anyone that wanted a divorce had to prove their spouse committed adultery or was otherwise relentlessly cruel in their treatment of the other spouse. In a 2010 Pew / Time magazine poll, it was revealed that 4 out of every 10 Americans think that marriage is becoming obsolete.

Did Mankind create divorce? What do you think about divorce? I will always believe that **NO FAULT DIVORCE,** was created by man. Was this the right thing to do? No, of course not! Why, because men have hardened their hearts!

Now we are seeing between 45 and 55 percent of all marriages end in divorce (depending on what part of America you live in). What is worse is that 67 percent of second marriages will end in divorce and 74 percent of third marriages will end in divorce. Today in America, about 25 to 30 percent of adults are divorced. Tragically, more than 1 million children each year in America will experience the breakup of a family through divorce! Even more disturbing is that the divorce rate may be lower than it was 20 years ago, not because there are fewer married people divorcing, but because people are living together outside marriage. **Before a man and woman are married should they talk about divorce?** As a writer of this book, **I think divorce should be a subject for marriage counseling!**

DIVORCE AND THE EFFECT ON CHILDREN

The heart-breaking facts about divorce (*this includes cohabitation divorce*) is how it affects the children. Children that have to go through a divorce have a 30 to 50 percent chance of having life issues such as depression to a point that they may need to be medicated, and let's hope not. They are more likely to be involved in crime, and alcoholism much younger in life. They also tend to abuse drugs which can lead to addiction or overdose, to steal because of poverty, and to have sex at an early age with the risk of STDs. Worst of all, the child may face the possibility of life without love. More often than not, these children grow up not being taken to church or programs, due to cost, where they could experience love from others. This might happen as well, these children can and will become unsociable if not taught to be sociable.

This happens to an innocent child because either or both the man and woman took their eyes off the plan for marriage and broke the covenant as the husband and wife. Has Satan, the thief come to steal, kill and destroy? Let's ask why are couples are allowing something, to destroy their family? Breaking the covenant of marriage opens the door for mistakes that destroy the family.

Children without guidance because of divorce, will not avoid the temptations that chase them through life, just because two parents did not keep their marriage covenant. The same could be said about cohabitation divorce.

This is the outcome of divorce and you are right to think it is tragic and sad! The facts in this chapter give the real meaning to the statement, <u>**"Divorce is like living in hell!"**</u>

<u>THE NEW AMERICAN TREND IN DIVORCE</u>

As if all the above wasn't a surprise, there is a new trend here in America. Those who have little regard for the real heartbreak of a failed marriage are having parties to celebrate divorce! They are called **DIVORCE PARTIES**. In past years divorce was a subject associated with shame, regret and remorse. Since or around 2000, divorce is not only rampant and out of control, it is being celebrated.

It gets worse. Newly divided families are having get-togethers or parties with friends and family members. They even go out on the town and celebrate the divorce. They may even have a large gathering at a cookout with drinks and gifts. They don't realize that the only gift they have received is from Satan and it will last for years to come.

The kicker of divorce parties is that the people throwing them and attending them think it makes the separation of divorce easier. <u>**NOTHING COULD BE FURTHER FROM THE TRUTH!**</u> They even believe it helps the children cope with the idea of Mom and Dad splitting up. How false is this? A broken marriage is still a broken family. The biggest divorce party will not change the reality of divorce! No matter what the party costs, the cost of divorce is enormous and goes on for years.

Another sad fact of a divorce party is the false belief that children are less traumatized if Mom and Dad continue a good relationship after the separation. According to a 2005 poll, even a good divorce causes psychological trauma to children and has effects that last into their adulthood. Does our western society glorify the divorce that destroys our families and children?

As families fall apart, any nation will fall apart as well! It is the family structure that reinforces a country and church. Ancient Rome is a good example of what will happen to a nation with widespread family breakdowns (*sickness and wars*) and divorce. Most historians note that the breakdown of the family was one of the symptoms, of the fall of the Roman Empire. This has also been seen in the USA, would you agree?

Today's, news media have countless articles describing how **young people** (children, teenagers and young adults) in fatherless homes, tend to turn to alcohol, drugs, illicit sex and crime far more often than children raised in established families. It's not hard to see the effects on America even as divorcees celebrate their divorces.

So, not only does the family suffer, but this country as a whole is suffering the consequences of divorce! Where is the country headed? If the family structure is broken by divorce, so will be the foundation of America. The real effect of no-fault divorce in this country is that they are turning America into an ungodly nation. Think of the consequences before you think about divorce!

I have left something to reveal to you at the end of this topic. That gift from the divorce party, may not be understood at the time it was given. Yet, the evidence will remain for years to come. Once opened, it cannot be put back in the box! This so-called gift, from the divorce party contains nothing, but sorrow! Now, you can understand what is really in that gift of a divorce and it can never be returned.

The reality of divorce is costly in many ways for men and women, and they tend to misunderstand the realism of the price tag caused by divorce and the cost of child support. **People that go through divorce never take into consideration the cost and how it will affect their budget!** This will last until the children are 18 years old or older.

Now, with that said, each of the parents will have to pay for housing and utilities, food, hygiene products, car Insurance, taxes and all the other issues during the lifetime of their children; like sports, music lessons, vacations, birthdays and holidays. This is one, if not the greatest reason why single adults are broke! **Welcome to the financial nightmare after a divorce that destroys family values!**

You should talk to people that have gone through divorce before you get a divorce! **I STRONGLY SUGGEST YOU REPAIR YOUR MARRIAGE BY REBUILDING YOUR FRIENDSHIP IN YOUR MARRIAGE!** Most married couples fail in this area of friendship or perhaps they never were friends, nor do they know how to rebuild the friendship within a marriage!

Most of the time, it takes only one person in a marriage who is not keeping the commitment of their marriage to bring about a divorce! The only thing that causes divorce is when one or both spouses take their eyes off their covenant blessing of the marriage. At this point they are opening the door to the temptations that bring sin into the marriage. When sin destroys a marriage, divorce is the tragic result. Do not ever forget the power of repentance, even when sin, mistakes and mismanagement, has stepped into a marriage. Repentance is a gift of love that brings blessings to your family.

After reading this chapter, could you have written out some of the effects on the family, young adults, children and America, after a divorce?

PART 10

I Lost My Spouse

After my divorce, I felt so unworthy and I did not want to be a friend to anyone or have a lady friend, and dating for me was out of the question! Sounds so familiar doesn't it? Divorce is hard on people and fills their mental state of mind full of resentment and a hardened heart.

Here are two issues after a person has lost their spouse, they will have to face? If they had a great marriage, they tend to hang on to that marriage for a long time. If they have a bad marriage, they feel like they don't want anything to do with another person or marriage. **Death and divorce of a spouse has some similarities and yet are so different.**

The point I want to bring up is getting people back into life and allowing them to understand it's OK to have a friend to do things with. I will be the first to say, you can build friendship and go out with someone without calling it a date or dating. I think it would be well advised to do so. **I also want you to know, you do not need to ask anyone if having a friend is OK!**

There are a lot of people, more so, people that are older, that only wish they had a friend. These single adults do not want a relationship because of the pain of losing a spouse or they had a bad experience within the relationship. I had ladies that I have gone out with and kept it within the rim of building friendship only and to this day we are still friends. That's a blessing for me and it should be a blessing for you!

Friends make a person feel important and wanted; they should be a part of ones' social life. This is how we stay friendly and how we show signs of caring for other people. Without friends you may become a dysfunctional person full of anger and live an apathetic lifestyle. I know, I used to be this kind of person.

I am not the first one to say, after your recovery time, go and have some fun; you owe it to yourself! Besides the community, people, friends, and love ones want you to have an enjoyable life. **A person must work through their past to have a real life!** We all need friends and there are people looking to be friends only. You could help someone that has been through the same thing as yourself. I wrote this book, due to my divorce and broken relationships.

<u>**This is a note from my friend and one of the editors of this book.**</u> *When losing a spouse due to death some people get lost in their grief and choose to stay there (in grief) and others may move forward avoiding the pain of grief. To stay in grief is a decision just as to work through grief is. We have no control over the reality of death, but we do have a choice of how we deal with it!*

One reason of not dealing with grief is, it is too painful. A reason of not moving on in life is that the person may feel afraid that they will forget their loved one or they may feel they are being disloyal to their deceased spouse. A person may even feel guilty if they choose to begin to allow themselves to develop a friendship or relationship. It is no more wrong than it was to develop the relationship they shared with their spouse.

We are all here to help each other live our lives as God would want us to. You should not let the loss determine your future. You should not be defined by what happen to you, but what you choose to become. **REMEMBER GOD WOULD WANT YOU TO CELEBRATE THE LOVE NOT THE LOSS.**

If you were to be asked and you are being asked, should a person have a life with a new friend after divorce or a spouse that has passed away? Instead of answering this question for yourself, how would you relate this question to someone you know that is a quality person that lives in grief, sorrow or regret? Every day we have a chance to help someone, make someone happy, and even make this world a better place to live. Give this book to someone that has lost their spouse. This book builds a person up to have a great relationship.

TEARS IN THE SAND

A tear fell into the sand,
just one of many that will fall.
The pain of life can make a person
stand upright and so tall.
The sand may absorb the tears,
but the memories may also remain.
A broken spirit, some say,
is much like a broken chain.
Memories that race within a person's mind,
at times has no place to hide.
But it's the choices and tides that keeps
my weary eyes open wide.
So, I chose to write the pain into the sand,
thoughts of the past.
The memories of love and relationships
that will always last.
I am sure it has and can be said,
in many ways and any day.
Walking on a beach can cleanse a person's thoughts,
in a solitary way.
As salt has cleanse many a wound,
though it's also painful to use.
Great memories will never go away,
they are the ones we choose not to lose.
Memories were never designed for pain either,
but to bring forth a smile.
Whether here or there, somehow,
we choose to stay for a while.
Yet the tears that have fallen on the beach,
cannot be counted by woman or man.
Whomever weeps tears in the sand,
will receive a harvest and learn to understand.
Write a thought on the sandy beach,
as you walk with a walking stick.
Leave the pain of a memory written on
the beach that your heart has picked.

Let your heart and mind be healed
by the crashing sounds of the waves.
That's the reason why we have tears in the sand,
it's a hidden treasure that saves.
Allow all your tears be counted as a blessing,
do you dare to leave tears in the sand?

By: Bill E. Carter
Owensboro KY
1/20/2020

PART 11

To The Teens

Don't think I left you out! I have had a lot of teenagers who have read my column, *"Today's Christian Singles."* Now, I would like to write to them on a personal level here. This book is also written for teens, so they would have the chance to view dating and courtship with knowledge and truth!

ADOLESCENTS OR TEENAGERS – I REFER TO THEM AS, ADULTS UNDER CONSTRUCTION! You may think it's your life and you're going to do what you want. That could be true and a big mistake at the same time. What if you had the knowledge to have a real friendship that turns into a loving relationship and a greater marriage? Teens, should come to understand that real relationships take time to build. How many mistakes are you going to make without this type of knowledge and information? *This book offers you a chance to read about common mistakes and maturity. So, before you do it your way, wouldn't it be better to listen to what this book has to offer and allow you to rethink it over first?*

Teens you have computer knowledge and I strongly suggest that you go online and study the four temperaments and take a temperament test. Just to find out your temperament and other types of temperaments. This will help teens understand and make changes in their behaviors and character. While you are at it, write down your bad habits. If you do not do this now, you may never face the truth about who you really are and the changes you need to make to have a real mature life!

I want you to understand what love is and I have outlined the real meaning of love throughout this book, which is achieved through time, trust, truth, faith, and friendship.

Sex is not love! Teenagers need to know that many people consider a relationship like a baseball game and brag about getting to first base. Be aware of this trash talk, when simple minded people speak. They will try to tell you what they think you want to hear, to achieve their sexual behavior.

Simple Minded: having or showing very *little intelligence* or *judgment*.

If you are in a sexual relationship and have expectations and imagination that this will be the person you spend the rest of your life with, then stop the sexual relationship and see what happens. Either they will want to have a lifetime relationship or just want a sexual relationship. Time will reveal the truth. This is where you need to take the steps of having that lifetime relationship built on time, trust, truth, faith, and friendship. Would you want to spend the rest of your life with someone who is not your best friend?

I want you to understand there are a few ways to contact an STD, and one way to get pregnant. We are at a time in American history when STDs in teenagers, teenage pregnancy, and adults with STDs, are near the same level as a third world country with this issue. Do you as an adult and teen, except this as a true statement?

The majority of teenagers with STDS, or pregnant teenagers, are at greater risk of having a poorer position in life, and a much lower quality of life. Were you aware of that? **Only about 25 percent of teenagers who find themselves with these issues will have a happy or satisfying life!**

Sex is not saying, "I love you." Becoming pregnant or contacting a STD is not saying, "I love you." These two tragedies for teenagers are happening at a rate of 30 percent in 2015, and will climb to 40 to 45 percent within the next 10 years, or by the year 2025.

Before you kiss someone and before you have sex, REALIZE THAT THERE IS NO SAFE SEX! One mistake, one temptation can and has change the course of many teenager's lives forever! Diseases, Flu, Germs, and STDs, can be pass on by kissing.

It is a well-known issue that teens have expectations and imaginations confused with reality and so do adults! This is why teen's parents, aunts, uncles, loved ones, and friends try to warn them about the steps they are taking. This guidance is given with love. If teens cannot understand that, they will not be able to see the real truth of love, in the relationship they are trying to have! (*Now at this point, remember the two cares.*)

Teens, have you ever heard an adult or maybe even a teenager say, *"I wish I had it to do all over again,"* or *"I wish I was young again"*? These are statements from people who have made mistakes in their life. Perhaps they stepped into a wrong relationship, a bad marriage, or suffered a difficult time after divorce. They may have become pregnant too young or contracted an STD that they could not get rid of.

Here is a statement I hear too often; "I married a stranger or I married the wrong person"! There are many reasons why people say, **"I WISH I HAD IT TO DO ALL OVER AGAIN."** Teenagers may not "hear" or understand the full effect of the sorrow hiding behind that statement. This statement of sorrow may follow a person throughout his or her entire life! Can you imagine that, at your young age? It happens every day!

The word "teenager" can refer to someone immature as well as someone in a certain age group. When adults use such statements as, **"You're a young adult,"** they are really saying that this young person is trying to be more mature! I like to use the phrase, **"adults under construction."** I think it helps to bring teenagers to the brim of being more mature. **We have adults older than 18 and well into their 30s, who still act like "teenagers." Please do not be this type of person.**

If you think or say as a teen or an adult, "It's my way or the highway," my suggestion to you is this. Pick up a Bible to use it as a road map to help you along life's highways.

PART 12

Basic Sex Education

THE PHYSICAL ACTION OF DATING!

THIS IS FOR ADULTS ONLY.
CAN BE READ BY ADOLESCENCE WITH THEIR PARENTS.

**What are your teens hearing in school,
social media, and on the streets of this nation?**
*This may stop a pervert from having sex with a
minor, spreading STDs, and false facts!*

I write this topic with the world and worldly people in mind and not from a Christian point of view. These thoughts and opinions came from my experiences, people from the singles program and issues that I know happen in everyday life. Parents why don't you share this topic and give them your opinion on this needed information. THIS IS RATED "RM": FOR REALITY AND MATURITY.

Now let's look more into the straightforwardness of sex. Let me set up the reality stage of sexuality. I SHARE THIS PART OF THE BOOK WITH ALL DUE RESPECT TO THE READER. I've done my best to write within reality, the truth and the mistakes, I have seen, learned, heard about and made.

What is sex: Sex is any physical action between a man and woman that stimulates the male and female organs, by touching, oral, or intercourse.

Kissing to a point where it stimulates the man and woman, can and will lead to touching and or pressing the body's sex organ against the male and the female that could cause a climax, which can leave the man wanting more and the women in emotional desire. (This can be done with clothing on.) This in the 50's and 60's was called making out and it's still is a type of making out and is sexual. This can lead to unwanted sexual intercourse, rape (date rape), STDs and becoming pregnant. This may also cause the male and female to masturbate.

From this point on, I will call masturbation, SOLO SEX: Solo sex, is sex by oneself, without a partner. This happens with the male and female, and it starts at an early age from 11 to 14 years old and lasts throughout adulthood.

Sex outside of marriage leaves most women disappointed and with men they seem like they do not care, **IT'S JUST SEXUAL ACTION**. Women will have sex, thinking this will make men love them. Men can and may try to just have sex as a challenge or action with a woman and eventually move on to other women. It may take a few adult years for a man to realize the value of a love filled sexual relationship. Men and Women that want sex outside of marriage have stepped into some of the I do not care stages of a relationship. I know that sounds bold but it's full of truth, isn't it?

Who gets hurt after a sexual relationship has ended? It's always one of the two isn't it? Only a few couples will walk away as friends after having sex, why?

What happens when man and woman have sex outside of marriage? There are a few issues that happen, within this physical lifestyle of sexuality. Let's look at these issues that I have learned over the course of my mistakes and other people who have talked about their issues within this lifestyle. I'm going to be transparent in these next issues. So, hold on to your thoughts, before you judge the book.

What is sex to a woman? When a woman has sex with a man for the most, she may think she has given everything she has to that man, even her heart or to say her love. Women may think they love men when they become sexual in a relationship. This may be only lust, let's be clear about this sexual action between a man and woman outside of marriage. We should know when it's lust only.

To a man, is sex just a physical action with no love in mind? A man can have sex and sometimes a woman, without any type of love or feelings for the other person! Remember this, it takes a man at least up to six months to understand if they even like a person.

I have looked up the word **Lust**: noun, very strong sexual desire, verb, have a very strong sexual desire for someone. **Lust** is a psychological force producing intense wanting for an object, or circumstance fulfilling the emotion. Lust can take any form such as the lust for sexuality, money or power. It can take such mundane forms as the lust for food as distinct from the need for food.

SOMETHING ABOUT ROMANCE AND SEX

ROMANCE AND SEX: Yes, there can be romance or being turned on before having sex. **Within marriage the desire to have sex for the most, is bonding to each other for life, this is where making love, so to speak, comes into reality.**

When sexual activities are done within the rim of romance, it is a pleasure to both the man and the woman. The man must learn how to make sexual activity romantic, for the woman to reach her desires and climax. It does not take much for a man to reach his orgasm or spasm. A spasm is where a man does not please the woman sexually and leaves her wanting more. **SPASM**: **S**exual **P**ractice **A**ctivity **S**pawning of a **M**an, who does not know how to treat a woman sexually! Men ask your wife, what she needs, to reach her climax when you get married and learn this!

Every man and woman choose to have sex, so why do most people get hurt emotionally about this physical action. Here's my two reasons why. After sex, the man thinks in many ways he owns the woman and the woman thinks she owns the man. This may be due to mating, the mating for life effect. Are humans to mate for life?

What is Monogamy: the practice or state of being married to one person at a time. If there is a break up after a sexual relationship for the most, all emotions, will be in disarray, confusion, dismay, disorder, panic, and madness. Does this happen? Every day would be my adult answer, what's yours?

When a man penetrates a woman that has never had sex, she loses her virginity and she bleeds both physically and emotionally. Then, when a woman has sex with a man it's always an emotional matter after sex, if she is not married! Why is this, men?

I believe it's because men and women are to mate for life, what are your thoughts? Possibly this is part of mankind's mindset or make up, to mate for life. This is why I think there is so much confusion in sex outside of marriage. Yes, that's my opinion! I cannot find another way to point this out or to understand why people get hurt after having sex outside of marriage. Do you have a better answer?

AGREEING TO HAVE SEX AS ADULTS: This happens and needs to be understood with maturity. Someone will become hurt over this matter and the embarrassment will follow. Yes, there are people who call themselves sex buddies or partners. But it's much like solo sex, this just leaves a person feeling empty or shameful. If these people do not feel remorse, I assure you, they will have sex with anyone. Here are a few thoughts to recap within this activity; what real enjoyment is there and what will happen when this partnership ends? **If adults do not have remorse, then how can they be trusted?**

SWINGERS: This is also full of STDs. There is no value or trust in this sexual act!

SOLO SEX: This is common within adolescents and adults. Parents, teach your teenagers about this and how they need to control this issue and how they should not do this while thinking about someone that they know. Teach them, if you must, not to overexert this. This can be a habit-forming issue. Boys and men will have solo sex more than girls and women. This is nothing to be ashamed of, unless, it becomes a bad habit or within the rim of being perverted.

STDs: STDs can come from anyone, at least 30% of our teens and adults, have or had an STD. Some STDs can be treatable, others remain for life. There is embarrassment and the dreadful issues that the STD may last a lifetime. There is no safe sex, condoms can and have failed.

SEXUALITY THAT IS ABNORMAL

Here is a reality check on a needed topic and one that needs to be understood. What is the nature of sex, most of us have never been taught this concept? Most people think it is just having a climax; but for the most, it's just something short of a spasm, or maybe at best, just sexual stress reduction and lust. The desire to have sex is real; how does a person keep a handle on this craving? Humans have never tried to control the temptation part of this. In the old days, parents would keep their daughters away from boys and young men. Did that work? To a point, but this created isolation and maybe even young men and ladies, to explore solo sex or same sex activity.

I also want to add that older people, both men and women when being turned off by the opposite sex their thoughts may turn to experimenting with the same sex. I did not write that to condemn people that are gay. I respect gay people; however, I do not believe in this behavior. Sex is always by choice, unless it's rape! I apologize if this offends anyone, I like to have the right to speak and write within my thoughts and understanding of the nature of sex.

Here's a note to have for understanding: Older men and women, may step into the gay culture to experiment or to find a new outlet to satisfy their sexual activities.

ORAL SEX: You can still get an STD from this act and is one step away from having intercourse. Oral sex is not by any means the natural way to have sex, I know of people that have repented from this sexual act. With that said, if you want to have oral sex, I feel it's up to the man or woman, to agree on what they want and do within the act of sexuality. *Some women do not like a man's fluid in their mouth and that should be respected.* Please note, some people view this as being perverted and some people do not.

ANAL SEX: This is not at all natural and somewhat perverted to me as a man. Most people would think this as well. However, there are women that like this sex behavior as well as men. **<u>ALLOW ME TO GIVE YOU A STRONG WARNING IF YOU ARE HAVING ANAL SEX.</u>** Men do not place your penis in the vagina of a woman after entering the anus; this can cause a woman to become infected. Anal sex can also cause the man's penis to become infected, take this as a warning as well. Repetitive anal sex may lead to weakening or tearing of the anal muscles, making it difficult to hold a person feces, which can cause stool leakage and the possibility of requiring a person to wear pads in the future.

If you receive anal sex be prepared for tearing, bleeding, and another opportunity to get a serious infection or STD or both! You should share this information with your friends, teenagers and loved ones. There are a lot more people than you think, that do not like this sexual behavior. **<u>I AM SPEAKING FROM A STRONG OPINION; A PERSON'S ANUS WAS NOT MADE FOR SEXUAL PLEASURES.</u>**

SEX PREDATORS: A sexual predator is a person seen as obtaining or trying to obtain sexual contact with another person in a metaphorically "predatory" or abusive manner. Analogous to how a predator hunts down its prey, so the sexual predator is thought to "hunt" for his or her sex partners. Adults and teens, be careful there are online predators.

Pedophile: An adult who is sexually attracted to or engages in sexual acts with, teens, children, toddlers or infants.

An act of a pedophile, must be reported to police at once. If you do not report this, they may seek other underage people. If you see or know something say something! Your strength and courage, will help protect someone else.

Porn: This is more than movies, magazines, books, etc. It teaches teens and adults, not to care about having one sex partner and it destroys the mindset of having real commitments. This is my opinion: This has and will cause people to think they can have sex with anyone. People that are addicted to porn, often think about having sex with someone that has no interest in them. They often get turn on so to speak, just by the opposite or same sex, that's just being friendly.

They create their own out of control sex behaviors that turn into addiction. The real effect is that porn can turn people into a perverted person. Perverts are never satisfied just with one person; they often masturbate a few times a day. They may ask and seek that their sex partner perform ungodly acts of sex, due to their out of control sex behavior. This is one addiction that is hard to overcome!

Teens that watch porn, without being taught sex education, may think this is normal. This could lead into a destructive lifestyle without any commitment. This may haunt them for life! *Parents have you asked your teens if they have watched porn?*

A word of warning to parents, these I-pods, and phones that open the door to the internet and web sites, may lead a person to think that porn is normal. **Parents, most teens have been exposed to porn; did you know that?**

Music: If you are not concern about what type of music they are listening to (*sex rap or gangster rap*) then their chances of watching porn and become addicted is the next thing that happens. **PORN HAS NO VALUE WHEN IT COMES TO FAMILY AND MORAL VALUES, DOES IT?**

STAYING WITHIN YOUR AGE GROUP: This is a wise thing to do and if you do not, someone will get hurt, or misled! Older people (*more so men*) look for younger people to mislead, to control, use for sex, or they want to feel young again. I am one, who thinks it's not right to have sex or date a person out of your age group. I leave that up to you to make this decision. If you married someone that is ten to fifteen years older or younger than you, the divorce rate is really high, it may be greater than 65% and that is also my opinion! Check the facts if you are a sugar daddy or gold digger.

I have found that parents haven't talked about these issues, with their adolescent. They may even assume their teens know enough about sex behavior and this is far from the truth. You become aware when the adolescent makes a mistake. Parents, it's time to speak with knowledge and guidance. What do our teenagers know about sex and is it the truth? I will assure you that teens do not really understand sex? Did you understand sex as a teenager? This needs to be talked about instead of it being taken for granted or ignored!

PART 13

Women Must Learn to Protect Themselves

This is something I would like to address to protect girls and women. Women you have the right to do and dress anyway you want to. The way females dress or act may give out unwanted and unintentional signals or messages to any given male. A man that is immature or just a pervert, may mistake or think your acting sexy and want sex, by your actions and dress style. What thoughts are you given out when you dress the way you do?

PLEASE TAKE NOTE OF THIS: Why do women wear the type of clothing that has their butt cheeks or breast exposed? Are women doing this to be viewed by the public and male factors?

Is this style of dressing, giving the wrong messages or is this a type of perverted act? Are you stating, "hey look at me"? Perverts will look at you when you dress provocatively! Women, do you want a perverted husband? A perverted husband or wife, may be a spouse that cannot be trusted, what's your thoughts?

Could this dress style make a man to overwatch a woman and perhaps make unwanted advancements? A man at this point may desire to talk with a female to check her intentions out. If a woman is dressing sexy is that a perversion? I hope this question allows a woman to rethink why man may make unwanted advances. This paragraph, was written so I could share with you a true statement; *"Your appearance can put forth an attitude"*. Attitude: In psychology, an attitude is an expression of favor or disfavor toward a person, place, thing, or event.

Moms and dads, as your teenage girls are physically developing, they should not be wearing the type of clothing (tights) that show the silhouette of their body and their breast exposed, much less their butt cheeks, hanging out, should they? Do you want your daughters to have sex, become pregnant or contact, one of the many STDs? *Is this what you want Moms and Dads?* LET'S ALL PUT SOME MORAL VALUES BACK INTO OUR ADOLESCENCE, AS PARENTS!

I assure you, teenagers are not ready for sex, so why allow them to step into this arena of sexual appearances and behaviors? If you allow your daughter to dress provocatively and they become pregnant or pickup an STD, should the blame rest on both parents as well as the adolescent? TEENAGERS ARE NOT ADULTS, REMEMBER THIS STATEMENT, MOMS AND DADS! **SHOULD DRESSING MODESTLY, BE TAUGHT AGAIN?**

Let's all think a little deeper about this matter. What if, your teenager that dresses so revealing, gets kidnaped for sex trafficking because of the way they are dressed or dressing? Is this a fear factor, or just a statement of concern? Surely you did not overlook this matter, have you? Do not become a parent that thinks we live in a secured country, or do you? Human trafficking is modern-day slavery and involves the use of force, fraud, or coercion to obtain some type of labor or commercial sex act.

Rape: Rape is a type of sexual assault usually involving sexual intercourse or other forms of sexual penetration carried out against a person without that person's consent. The act may be carried out by physical force, coercion, abuse of authority, or against a person who is incapable of giving valid consent, such as one who is unconscious, incapacitated, has an intellectual disability or is below the legal age of consent. The term *rape* is sometimes used interchangeably with the term *sexual assault*.

PUBLIC PLACE

How does a woman avoid being raped? Those first few dates you should meet in a public place; this could help! Come to know a person when you first meet someone and that takes time. Women, never go to the man's home or apartment without understanding some of their behavior and character issues. **It would be wise if the woman and man, has a discussion on what they want out of this relationship they are trying to have.**

Make sure women that you ask the right question. Women, before you go out with a man ask them about their sexual mindset. Women, most men want to have sex, some are more up front then others, so be very aware of this! We have been taught this behavior of sexuality and no one really tries to un-teach this behavior. The public sees and is exposed to sexuality every day and all day long. This just confuses mankind, doesn't it?

DOING ACTIVITIES BY YOURSELF IN A PUBLIC PLACE: It's hard to make every public place a safe zone; women need to understand this! Do not place yourself in the un-safe zone! Women should learn to have a battle buddy (a trusted friend that knows what you are doing). This is a must within today's society! Are we living in a world where everyone is friendly? **REMEMBER, YOUR ACTION MAY CAUSE A REACTION!**

LEARN SELF-DEFENSE: This is a good workout anyway. Learn to stop a person who reacts with un-wanted advances or threats both verbally and physically! This should be a teaching for girls and women! Carry some pepper spray (or a weapon).

PART 14

Rape Prevention

I want people to understand, rape is a perverted action and I think it's demonic! If rape gives you power and control of a person and if this makes you feel sexually excited, you are not in control of your mind. You are living with your out of control imagination. If you have this issue get help! Our daughters and sons of America, do not need to be raped!

I want you and everyone to understand, there are plenty of people to have sex with. If you want sex, all you have to do is, put your appearance into check, clean up, be friendly and if you are seeking a sex partner, seek one with their knowledge. I assure you; you will find someone to have sex with and sooner than you think! **THERE IS NO NEED TO RAPE!**

When a woman talks with a man or when a person smiles at someone, they are only being friendly. **Don't allow your mind to think everyone wants to have sex with you.** Please understand this and become a responsible person. Go back and read how to be a friend and what it is to be a companion and compatible.

YOU ARE THE ONLY ONE THAT CAN KEEP YOURSELF FROM RAPING A PERSON! A person must learn to control their perverted acts. Companionship and friendship, is not always about sex. Women, people that are having sex with you may not be a friend, this could very well be a person with a sexual addiction.

I want to give a word of warning here. Do you know men, who think they can have sex with any woman at any given time of the day? That is a perverted person and by all means, place that person back into reality by asking that person to get help and counseling. Men do not leave a man un-checked in this action or thought. This may help a woman from being raped.

MEN, MOST WOMEN WOULD NOT HAVE SEX WITH YOU AT ALL! So, *stop thinking that every woman wants to have sex with you!* It certainly doesn't hurt to ask a person if they are a pervert; this may put their thoughts into captivity. I'm asking men to step up on this problem.

If you are intimidated in seeking a sex partner, you need to learn how to advance your people skills. If you meet someone and all you want is just sex, share with that person that you are seeking a sex partner and perhaps a friend. Do not be improper in this matter at all, and never do this at work.

Nevertheless, if this is talked about up front, then everyone is on the same page. Some people only want sex and not a relationship, yet they can become some type of acquaintance.

A person does not have to rape a person to have sex! if a person shares with you, they are not looking for this type of affair, which is their right, understand this statement; **"NO MEANS NO!"**

There are a lot of people looking to have a sexual encounter. Learn to develop your speaking and people skills. You will find by having the permission of someone to have sex with, will give you a greater climax. Isn't this what you are looking for anyway? Do not be stupid, out of control, or demonic. There is no real need for that, is there! Rape is an evil act; if you need help, seek counseling for this sexual behavior!

If you have been raped report this as soon as you can, and get medical help. Buy reporting this you could save another person from being raped. We can stop rape if we all work together!

PART 15

Stepping Out on Your Own

I wanted to add this to help protect you, as you leave home and seek to start your adult life. When you leave home, most people begin work, trade school, college or the military. You are stepping out on your own for the first time. I know some of the troubles you can face, for I left home when I was sixteen. Yet, I want to talk to you about leaving home.

At 18 years old or older you should be thinking about your future. Remember it's your life and now you should find the path of life you want to walk. What roads will you take? The faster you get yourself out of the house; the sooner you will learn about life and have your own life.

A question needs to be answered, are you mature enough? People will quickly say yes, but are they? The secret to stepping out on your own is finding the right vision you chose to walk on; keep the vision you have planned. We all know that partying is not a vision at all! A vision has value, which requires a person to have moral values, remorse, the knowledge of repenting and how to avoid mistakes. This in return gives us maturity and wisdom.

A vision must have the right goals. If you set goals that are not attached to a vision, you will never adjust the goal or goals to become the right goal and one within a set of goals that is applied to a vision.

Goal: A **goal** is an idea of the future or desired result that a person or a group of people envisions, plans and commits to achieve. People endeavor to reach goals within a determinate time by setting deadlines.

Personal Vision Statement: The vision statement that I want you to write about is a personal road map, that indicates what the person wants to become by setting a defined direction for their personal growth. Vision statements undergo minimal revisions during the course of the vision and may be updated from year-to-year. Your vision statement should be written down, so you may know which road to take to become successful!

PARTY LIFE

I want to expose the party life to you. Party life, will eat at your budget or even worse, you could be assaulted, raped and contact a STD. You can become addicted to partying. I WANT TO WARN YOU NOT TO STEP INTO THE ARENA OF NOT KNOWING THE TRUTH ABOUT WHAT CAN HAPPEN AT THESE SO-CALLED ADULT PARTIES. Here is part of a column I wrote called;

"The Addicted Americans"

The addicted Americans and the use of drugs and alcohol, has stolen more money, wasted so much time, wasted our nation's health, destroyed homes, families, and has brought shame upon many people! Who has paid for this destructive lifestyle? It has affected every American since drugs and alcohol was introduced by mankind since the dawn of time! Did you know that Americans use 80 to 90% (per CDC) of the pain medication that is produced in the world? What country is more addicted to drugs and alcohol?

Cigarettes and most tobacco products have a drug in them we call nicotine. Nicotine is a potent parasympathomimetic alkaloid found in the nightshade family of plants and is a stimulant drug. Nicotine is the main ingredient in tobacco products that can and will cause addiction.

One drink of alcohol and one hit or ("getting high on drugs"), and one use of a tobacco product laced with Nicotine can last a lifetime and we call this addiction! Perhaps half of the adults in America are addicted to some form of alcohol or drugs (that includes street and prescription medication).

What about the cost? Example: If your addiction is only $5.00 per day X 7 days = $35 x 4 weeks = $140 x 12 months = **$1680 per year** x 5 years = $8,400 (**20 years the cost is $33,600**) **and that is a low-cost addiction.**

What if your addiction was $10 or $15 per day? No wonder people are broke, all from the cost of addiction! What's sad is people allow themselves to become a slave to partying or addiction, and never know they lost their freedom? How does that drink taste now and how high do you have to get to forget you lost your freedom?

People that are addicted have to face their addiction master every day or weekend. This master of addiction smiles as he steals your money, love, family, home, and freedom? Do you party with your master of addiction? Are you strong enough to fight for your freedom or will you become defeated?

"You cannot talk to a drunk or someone who is stoned". **PEOPLE WHO ARE ADDICTED WILL NOT HEAR WORDS OF WISDOM!** Without wisdom or knowledge of the truth, people are destroying themselves. Sounds like America to me!

One mistake while you are intoxicated from drugs or alcohol, can kill, harm, and change the course of your life and others. The next thing we all hear is, I didn't mean to. Yes, you did! You have been warned for year after year not to do this. Here is another statement I hear, if I did not get buzzed up, I would not have done this. What a dumb statement!

How many good jobs have been lost due to this addiction of partying? How many people have chosen to party instead of finishing their trade school training or college education? How many people have ruined their education or military careers, due to partying?

Stepping into the work force, trade skills, college or the military, beware there are sexual predators waiting for you. Most of them are nice looking, perhaps it's someone you trust, someone that calls you a friend, or they could be a few years older than you. Most of all, there are those who will try to coach you into the area of "LET'S GO PARTY"! When people pull you into a mistake or sin, it's because misery love's company, would you agree? You may think it can't be wrong, because everyone is doing it. Nevertheless, the question remains, what are you going to do with the rest of your life?

What is worse than the above, our own parents have taught us to party, but they will not admit this, yet their children have watched them for years. You think, if it was good enough for Mom and Dad, then it must be OK. Before you turn on that party light, rethink what you want out of life. Do not let the lust of life pull you into the gates of hell. If you step into a party, are you going to be strong enough to walk out and find a real relationship?

With this book you can learn how time, truth, trust, faith and friendship will enable you to have the loving lifetime companionship, you are searching for.

Please, tell your friends and love ones, about this unique book on dating. You can buy this book by the cases and send it to a military base chaplain's office. They have a lot of young soldiers that need to read this! Buy this book for your neighborhood teenagers, this would give them something to do and learn!

SUPPORT OUR TROOPS!
By: Bill E. Carter 10/10/2018
Owensboro Kentucky

BE SAFE AND DO NOT HATE!

One of the editors and proofreaders, was 89 years old. She didn't want to be named. I wrote this poem for her. Thank you, my new friend.

BEHIND A KEYBOARD

Behind a keyboard,
I write.
Education, knowledge, wisdom and life experience,
sometimes I fight.
Songs, poems, short stories, short plays, and books,
have taught me.
Freedom is in one's mindset, yes,
the mind is a wonderful place to be!
I never would have learned to write,
if I did not read.
When I am alone or down, this gift of writing allows me to
hear and see.
I hear the words and I see the words and they lead me
down the road to truth.
Now I have grown old and have to un-fold somewhat,
like Jake, Jeannie, and Ruth.
I'm old now, with gray and white,
In my hair.
As I sit in my
favorite chair.
I can still unwind and unfold,
behind a keyboard.

I wrote this poem this morning, for my new friend listed above. A teacher that spent time with me as a writer, proofreading we did, sitting in her dining room. Thank you so much for helping me.

☺ By: Bill E. Carter 10/2019

Companionship

Couples in unity with companionship love
Oneness with their faith and love
May God bless us, in all of our years to come
Putting our hearts together to make a home
Affection and love that will never end
Never forget the time it took to be a friend
I always want you to be my best friend
Oh, I have every day to show you I care
Now that we have each other there is no fear
She and I have an everlasting relationship
Here we stand in love of our companionship
In our hearts rest faith, love and trust
Prayers that keep our love from turning to rust

By: Bill Carter
9/9/07

COMPANIONSHIP
GROUP BOOK
E- books & Paperbacks
Order at www.liferichpublishing.com

COMPANIONSHIP
GROUP BOOK
E- books & Paperbacks
Order at www.liferichpublishing.com

COMPANIONSHIP
GROUP BOOK
E- books & Paperbacks
Order at www.liferichpublishing.com

COMPANIONSHIP
GROUP BOOK
E- books & Paperbacks
Order at www.liferichpublishing.com

COMPANIONSHIP
GROUP BOOK
E- books & Paperbacks
Order at www.liferichpublishing.com

COMPANIONSHIP
GROUP BOOK
E- books & Paperbacks
Order at www.liferichpublishing.com

COMPANIONSHIP
GROUP BOOK
E- books & Paperbacks
Order at www.liferichpublishing.com

COMPANIONSHIP
GROUP BOOK
E- books & Paperbacks
Order at www.liferichpublishing.com

COMPANIONSHIP
GROUP BOOK
E- books & Paperbacks
Order at www.liferichpublishing.com

COMPANIONSHIP
GROUP BOOK
E- books & Paperbacks
Order at www.liferichpublishing.com

COMPANIONSHIP
GROUP BOOK
E- books & Paperbacks
Order at www.liferichpublishing.com

COMPANIONSHIP
GROUP BOOK
E- books & Paperbacks
Order at www.liferichpublishing.com

Just cut and tear out tab for online information. You can buy this book by the case to save cost. Please send books to our soldiers of any military base to: The Chaplin's Office. Thanks, Bill E. Carter.